This

Journal

Belongs To:

_____

If it's true life offers only three eventualities to anyone suffering from the disease of addiction: recovery/institutions, jail, or death; then we're all in trouble. Addiction is not just the addict's problem. It becomes a family problem, and eventually a societal one. There's no getting around that.

Some may be flinching at the use of the word 'disease' to describe addiction. But whether one agrees with it or not, the American Medical Association classified alcoholism as a disease back in 1975 and included drug addiction later in 1987. In addition, the Diagnostic and Statistical Manual (DSM-5) of the The American Psychiatric Association recognizes addiction as a diagnosable psychiatric disorder, describing it as:

"A chronic, relapsing disorder characterized by compulsive drug seeking, continued use despite harmful consequences, and long-lasting changes in the brain."

Those "long-lasting changes in the brain" are how the word disease is medically justified. Addiction literally changes the physiological landscape of the brain, so that the afflicted person no longer thinks the same way. And in late-stage addiction, they no longer look the same because like any disease, it takes a visible toll on one's body and mind, just as if it were cancer.

Still, regardless of whether you view substance abuse as a disease or not, one truth can't be denied: the increasing scourge of addiction on our streets, in our homes, and in our families, is epidemic. And for those who love someone, have a spouse, or have a son or daughter with addiction, watching them push away the help they need the most and succumb to their demons is heartbreaking. It's a slow, painful death to witness.

Gut wrenching.

Addiction creates grief daily, not only from watching the addiction steal your loved one from themselves, but from the grief one feels for the loss of a thousand-nurtured dreams once held for them with hope.

To love an addict is to grieve. Daily. It is a grief that is persistent and unrelenting.

Therefore, this guided journal is designed to serve as both an emotional outlet for your own pain, and as tool for healing, reflection, and growth. It is designed to help take some of that undeserved weight of addiction off your shoulders, because:

You didn't cause it, You can't control it, and You can't cure it.

Please read that again, because it's true.

Tattoo it into your soul.

This journal is also a place for you to take care of yourself, a safe space to express your feelings regardless if they're negative or positive. Don't define them as good or bad, just feel them and acknowledge them as part of yourself for the moment. It is a 7-day intense but healing deep dive into yourself as you exist in your relationship with your addicted loved one. These 7 days do not have to be completed consecutively but can be accomplished as tolerated. You are encouraged to repeat the journal as often as needed.

This is your place to be real with yourself. No one else matters here but you.

There will be days when you hate your addict for destroying their lives and everyone else's in the process. Get those words out of your head and heart and onto paper.

Once you do write those words you will find that you really *don't* hate your addicted loved one. You hate their addiction. You hate the drugs. And you hate what those drugs have done to them. The two have become so seemingly inextricably entwined that most days you can't tell where one begins and the other leaves off.

The deeper truth is, you know you love them and would be happy to have them back and in sustained recovery so they could leave the insanity behind and become whole again.

Because what's good about addiction?

NOTHING.

Here is an outline of topics to be covered:

1.Setting Intentions

Prompts: "What do I hope to gain from journaling through this experience?"
Reflection: A space for setting goals (e.g., self-care, emotional processing, understanding, acceptance).

2.Emotional Awareness

Daily Emotional Check-in:
- How am I feeling today? (with a range of emotions to circle.
- What triggered this emotion?
- How did I react to this feeling, and how could I handle it next time?

Prompts:
- "How has my loved one's addiction impacted me emotionally?"
- "What emotions am I struggling with most right now?"

3.The Biggie: Managing Guilt and Shame

Prompts:
- "In what ways do I feel responsible for my love one's addiction?"
- "How can I start to let go of feelings of guilt or blame?"

A section for affirmations to release guilt and focus on compassion toward oneself. Scream and cry too, if you need to.

4.Coping with Uncertainty

Prompts:
- "What uncertainties am I facing today, and how am I coping with them?"
- "What are the things within my control?"

Reflection Exercise: Write down fears and hopes, then identify actionable steps to reduce anxiety.

5. Practicing Self-Compassion and Self-Care

Prompts:
- "What about ME?"
- "What have I done for myself today?"
- "In what ways can I practice more self-compassion?"

Exercise: A self-care checklist to promote daily habits like exercise, relaxation, connecting with support groups, and nurturing hobbies.

6.Setting Boundaries, something we all need help with as the disease changes.

Prompts:
- "What boundaries have I set for my addicted loved one, and how do I feel about them.
- "How do I respond when those boundaries are challenged?"

Reflection: Understanding the importance of boundaries for emotional well-being and tips on maintaining them.

7. Gratitude in Difficult Times

Daily Gratitude Section: Write 3 things you're grateful for, even in hard moments.
Prompts:
- "What lessons has this experience taught me about myself and my relationships?"
- "Who or what has been a source of support?

8. Letting Go and Acceptance

Prompts:
- "What am I struggling to accept?"
- "How would letting go of certain expectations change my emotional experience?"

Exercise: Writing a letter of acceptance to oneself, acknowledging that the situation is beyond full control.

9. Hope and Resilience

Prompts:
- "What does resilience mean to me, and how have I been resilient so far?"
- "What small steps can I take today to foster hope for the future?"

Exercise: Creating a vision board for healing and hope in the back of the journal.

10. Support Network and Community

Prompts:
- "Who can I turn to for support when things feel overwhelming?"
- "How can I ask for help when I need it?"

Exercise: Writing a list of supportive people and community resources.

11. Reflections on Growth

Prompts:

- "Looking back, how have I grown through this journey?"
- "What positive changes have come from this experience?"

Other Sections

- Space for Free Writing
- Dedicated pages for unstructured thoughts, reflections, and personal expressions.

Additional Elements:

Quotes or Affirmations: Include comforting or motivating quotes related to healing, strength, and perseverance.

Mindfulness Practices: Suggestions for grounding exercises or breathing techniques to help parents navigate intense emotions.

Resources: Include information about support groups, therapy, or online communities for parents of addicts.

So let your journey toward health and away from insanity begin here. This journal will take you through one intense week of self-discovery and its resultant sanity, And like a refreshing shower also makes clean, repeat as needed!

Every journal is a journey, every journey is a life.

Day 1

What do I hope to gain from journaling through this experience?

_____
_____
_____
_____
_____
_____
_____
_____
_____
_____
_____
_____
_____
_____
_____

Set some self-care goals for yourself:

Date:

How am I feeling today: Happy Resentful Peaceful Sad Numb
Furious Defeated Guilty Angry Depressed Empty Anxious
Inspired Helpless Confused Held hostage Isolated

(Circle as many as are accurate)

Who or what triggered these emotions?

How did I react?

What emotions am I strugling with most now?

How has my child's addiction impacted me emotionally?

_____
_____
_____
_____
_____
_____
_____
_____
_____
_____
_____
_____
_____
_____

How can I handle it differently next time?

_____
_____
_____
_____
_____
_____
_____
_____
_____
_____
_____
_____
_____
_____

Notes

Managing Guilt & Shame

Managing guilt and shame when dealing with an addicted loved one can be incredibly challenging. These emotions are natural, but they can be overwhelming and detrimental to your mental health. Acknowledge and validate your emotions. This journal will help you accomplish this.

Accept that your feelings are normal because they are! You'd have to be crazy to tolerate some of the situations the addict creates. Remember that guilt and shame are common reactions when someone you care about is struggling with addiction, so it's important to validate that these feelings are part of the process.

Trying to ignore or bury guilt and shame will often intensify them. Find a healthy outlet, like this journal, or by talking to a therapist, or confiding in a trusted friend is essential.

Realize that addiction is a disease: Addiction is a complex condition, not a moral failing. Your loved one's addiction is not your fault, and understanding the science behind addiction can help alleviate feelings of guilt.

Separate the person from the addiction: Recognize that your loved one's actions while in addiction are influenced by their illness, and not a reflection of their true self.

◇ ◇ ◇

Remember, you are not responsible for "fixing" your loved one. Setting limits helps protect your own mental and emotional well-being. It can be difficult to say no, but healthy boundaries prevent you from being consumed by guilt. DON'T FEEL GUILTY ABOUT SETTING BOUNDARIES!

While you can offer support, focus on healing yourself. The path to recovery, for **both** you and your loved one, is a process that takes time, patience, and self-compassion.

Release the burden of guilt by practicing self-forgiveness. You cannot go back and change the past, but you can choose to move forward with more knowledge and compassion. This doesn't mean condoning harmful behavior, but letting go of resentment about it can free you from emotional pain.

Participate more fully on your own life. Your life needs more of YOU, and less of the addict.

In what ways do I feel responsible for my loved one's addiction?

_____

_____

_____

_____

_____

_____

_____

_____

How can I startt to let go of feelings of guilt or blame?

_____

_____

_____

_____

_____

_____

_____

_____

_____

_____

I am full of compassion towards myself.
I release the stories that make me feel small.
I hold space for myself in this healing process.
I deserve happiness

Notes

_____
_____
_____
_____
_____
_____
_____
_____
_____
_____
_____
_____
_____
_____
_____
_____
_____
_____
_____
_____
_____
_____
_____

Coping with Uncertainty

Uncertainty is the only thing we can be certain about when dealing with an addicted loved one. Their moods can change from one minute to the next and so can their irresponsible decisions. You may never be sure how the person will react in certain situations or whether they will keep promises.

Trust is often damaged by the dishonesty, manipulation, or betrayal that can accompany addiction. Rebuilding trust can be uncertain and takes time, and you may wonder if the person will ever be truthful or reliable again.

Addiction can lead to financial instability for the person suffering and for those around them. There can be uncertainties around how much support to offer, whether it will be misused, or if financial losses will affect long-term stability.

The future of someone battling addiction is often unclear. You may worry about their health, well-being, and ability to recover in the long term chronic effects. Will today be the day you get 'the call'?

Depending on the addiction, legal problems or dangerous situations can be highly unpredictable, whether it's related to illegal substances, DUIs, or other risky behaviors.

Then there is the uncertainty of answering the phone whenever it rings! Will they ask for money again? Be verbally abusive again? Threaten you again?

What uncertainties am I coping with today?

What are the things within my control and what can I do about them?

Refection Exercise

Write down both your fears and your hopes, then identify
actionable steps to reduce the anxiety of uncertainties. i.e.
yoga, exercise, refuse to answer the phone, etc.

Practicing Self-Compassion & Self-Care
What about YOU?

Loving someone with an addiction can be so incredibly challenging, that we forget about our own needs in favor of the addict's demands and inconsistencies. Therefore, it's twice as important and twice as difficult, to prioritize self-compassion and self-care. But our emotional lives depend upon it. Here are some helpful ways to love yourself:

- **Establish clear boundaries to prevent the addict's behavior from overwhelming your life**. Boundaries might involve limiting financial support, maintaining emotional distance when necessary, or refusing to engage in conversations when the person is under the influence.

- **Be kind to yourself in moments of emotional struggle**. Speak to yourself as you would to a friend in a similar situation, with understanding and care.

- **It can be helpful to have people who can listen without judgment.** Join Support Groups: Consider groups like Al-Anon or Nar-Anon, where you can connect with others who understand the complexities of loving someone with an addiction.

- **Engage in activities that nourish your mind, body, and spirit.** Whether it's exercise, meditation, journaling, or hobbies, self-care isn't selfish; it's necessary.

- **Maintain Routines:** Structure and routine can help you feel grounded. Continue focusing on your own goals and daily activities, even when the addict's behavior feels all-consuming.

- **Detach with love**. Detaching with love means caring for the person without feeling responsible for their choices or enabling their addiction. You can offer support, but their recovery is ultimately their responsibility.

- **Acknowledge your efforts.** Recognize the strength it takes to love someone with an addiction, and be proud of the steps you've taken to care for yourself. Celebrate small victories in maintaining your boundaries and emotional health.

No one is going to take care of you, but you! It sure won't be your addicted loved one. Keep this foremost in your mind, not as a source of resentment toward them but as a simple reality that needs to be honored.

What have I done for myself today?

_____

_____

_____

_____

_____

_____

_____

It what ways can I promote more self-compassion?

_____

_____

_____

_____

_____

_____

_____

_____

Self –Care Check List

Circle as many as needed

Relaxing bath   Hobby   Write an email

Exercise   Relaxation techniques

Support group   Counseling   Movie

Journal writing   Walk   Day trip

Talk with a friend   Out to eat

Yoga   Read   Watch TV

Add more:

_____

_____

_____

Setting Boundaries

Setting boundaries with addicted loved ones is crucial for several reasons, both for your well-being and theirs. Without boundaires, we are held hostage to someone else's addiction. We are stuck in their addiction with them. Here's why setting clear boundaries is important:

1. Protects Your Emotional and Mental Health
Addiction can create emotional chaos, leading to stress, anxiety, and burnout for family members and friends. Boundaries help maintain your mental health by giving you control over what behavior you will and will not tolerate. It allows you to keep a healthier emotional distance from destructive patterns.

2. Promotes Personal Accountability
By setting boundaries, you encourage the addicted person to take responsibility for their actions. If they experience the natural consequences of their behavior, they are more likely to realize the need for change. Enabling, on the other hand, can perpetuate the addiction.

3. Prevents Codependency
Without boundaries, there is a risk of falling into a codependent relationship where you prioritize their needs over your own. This dynamic can reinforce unhealthy behaviors and keep both of you stuck in a negative cycle.

4. Maintains Clarity on Support
Boundaries define what kind of help you are willing to offer (e.g., emotional support, helping find treatment) versus what you're not (e.g., giving money, covering for their behavior). This clarity prevents confusion and emotional manipulation.

5. Facilitates Recovery
Boundaries can motivate the addicted person to seek help. When they recognize that their actions have limits and consequences, they may be more inclined to pursue treatment. Boundaries are a form of tough love that signals you care but won't enable harmful behavior.

6. Prevents Financial and Legal Strain
Addiction can sometimes lead to financial or legal issues. Boundaries help protect you from being dragged into these problems, preserving your own stability and protecting against becoming entangled in their consequences.

7. Fosters Respect and Dignity
Boundaries can also reinforce the idea that everyone deserves respect, both the addicted person and yourself. Setting clear expectations of behavior fosters healthier interactions and mutual respect.

Boundaries are essential to protect both yourself and your loved one from the toxic effects of addiction, enabling you to support them in a healthier, more constructive way.

by Noelle Rousseau

I wish someone would have told me that sacrificing my boundaries in the name of empathy wasn't noble .
I wish they would've warned me that all it would do is make me a safe house for other people's demons .
I think empathy has to be taught in two parts.
How to put yourself in someone else's shoes and see the hurt they were given that made them hurt you & how to understand that you still don't deserve what they're doing .
Their scars are no excuse for the wound they give to you .
Their inability to heal is not something you can fix .
If you give them excuses and safe places for their darkness instead of demanding they do better,
the only thing you are teaching them is that you will put up with it .
We want to live in a world where hurt people don't hurt people .
But the reality is, that starts with standing up for yourself and not accepting disrespect .
You choose to heal.
You choose to take the darkness the world gave you and still be the light.
You choose kindness despite the pain you received .

They can too.

What boundaries have I set for my loved one and how to I feel about them?

_____
_____
_____
_____
_____
_____
_____
_____
_____

How do I respond when those boundaries are challenged?

_____
_____
_____
_____
_____
_____
_____
_____
_____
_____

Reflection:

Tips on maintaining boundaries

1. Clearly Define Your Boundaries

Take time to reflect on what behaviors you will and will not accept. Be specific and realistic about your limits. For example, you might set a boundary like, "I won't give you money, but I will help you find treatment options."

2. Communicate Boundaries Clearly

Once you've established your boundaries, communicate them to your loved one in a calm, direct, and compassionate manner. Make sure they understand what your limits are and what the consequences will be if those limits are crossed. You may have to write them down on paper to refer to if your loved one needs to be reminded. Texting those boundaries is also a good idea. These boundaries are not open for emotional negotiation.

3. Stay Consistent

This is a biggie, the linch pin on whether your boundary setting works or doesn't work. Consistency is key. If you waver on your boundaries, it sends mixed signals and may encourage manipulative behavior. Stick to your boundaries even if it's uncomfortable or your loved one pushes back.

4. Follow Through with Consequences

If your boundary is crossed, enforce the consequence you've communicated. For example, if you've said you won't lend money and they ask for it, remind them of your boundary and don't give in. DO NOT GIVE IN. Without consequences, boundaries lose their effectiveness.

5. **Practice Self-Care**

Maintaining boundaries with a loved one struggling with addiction is emotionally draining. Make sure you're taking care of yourself—whether it's through therapy, support groups, hobbies, or simply taking time for yourself to decompress. Healthy boundaries start with self-care. Repeat that. Healthy boundaries begin with self-care. Give yourself that much needed break from the chaos.

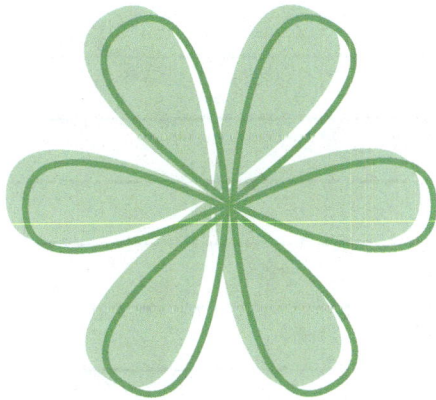

Notes

_____Date
_____
_____
_____
_____
_____
_____
_____
_____
_____
_____
_____
_____
_____
_____
_____
_____
_____
_____
_____
_____

Gratitude in Difficult Times

Creating gratitude during difficult times feels almost impossible, but it can be transformative, helping to shift your perspective and build resilience.

That said, It's not easy to feel graitude when your addicted loved one just stole your computer and hawked it for drugs. It's not easy to feel gratitude when you have to hide your charge cards every time the addict comes to visit. None of it is easy. Every bit of it is painful. But , that only makes gratitude more essential to keep you from sliding down that slippery slope into depression and despair and staying there. Your despair won't help you, and it sure won't help your addict. So, here are a few ways to cultivate gratitude when when genuine gratitude seems light-years away:

1. Focus on Small Wins
In difficult times, the big picture may seem overwhelming. Instead, focus on small achievements, even tiny moments of comfort or joy—a warm cup of tea, a supportive text, or even just getting through the day!

2. Practice Mindfulness
Mindfulness helps you stay present, and this awareness can bring attention to things you might usually take for granted. It allows you to see the small positive things that still exist, even in tough times, like a sunny day or the sound of birds.

3. Write It Down
Journaling can be an effective way to process emotions and practice gratitude. Even writing down one thing you are thankful for each day can shift your mindset over time, helping you notice the good around you. It retrains your brain to see the good.

4. Reframe Challenges

Try to see difficulties as opportunities for growth. Ask yourself, "What is this teaching me?" Finding lessons in hardships can foster a sense of appreciation for the personal growth that may emerge from them.

5. Gratitude Rituals

Incorporate daily gratitude rituals, like saying thank you aloud or reflecting at the end of each day on things you are thankful for. Over time, this trains your brain to look for positive moments even in adversity. Again, this takes time, so make it one of your habits for self-care.

6. Connect with Others

Expressing gratitude to others, even for the smallest gestures, builds a sense of connection and community. It can also help to surround yourself with people who uplift you, which makes it easier to find gratitude.

These steps won't remove the difficulties, but they can help shift your focus to the positive aspects of life, making tough situations more manageable. Soooooo.....

Thank you!

Write 3 things you are grateful for:

1 _____

2 _____

3 _____

What lessons has this experience taught me about myself:

_____

_____

_____

_____

_____

_____

_____

_____

Who or what has been a source of support:

_____

_____

_____

_____

Notes

Date

Letting Go & Acceptance

Acceptance and letting go do not mean condoning the addict's poor choices and self destructive behaviors. But they are both crucial for someone who loves an addict. Why? Because they allow the person to preserve in their own well-being while supporting the addict in healthier, more sustainable ways. Here's some other reasons why these two elements matter so much:

1. Recognizing Limits of Control

Addiction is a complex issue that can't be solved by love or force. No matter how much you care for someone, you can't control their behavior or choices. Letting go means accepting that the responsibility for their recovery lies with them, not you. It reduces feelings of helplessness and frustration when efforts to "fix" them don't work.

2. Setting Healthy Boundaries

Letting go doesn't mean abandoning the person; rather, it involves setting boundaries to protect your emotional and mental health. Accepting that you can't control their addiction allows you to establish limits on behaviors that are harmful to you or your relationship and creates space for healthier interactions without enabling the addict.

3. Emotional Freedom

Acceptance helps you release the intense guilt, anger, and fear that often accompany loving someone with an addiction. It enables emotional freedom by allowing you to focus on your own healing journey. By accepting the reality of the situation, you stop fighting against it and learn to manage your own emotions rather than being consumed by the addict's actions.

4. Empathy Over Judgment

Letting go of the need to control or change the addict can foster more compassion and empathy. Acceptance helps you see addiction as a disease, not a moral failure. This shift can improve the way you relate to the person, focusing more on understanding and support rather than frustration or blame. And yes, it's difficult!!

5. Support Without Enabling

When you accept the situation for what it is, you're better able to offer meaningful support. Letting go of the idea that you can rescue the addict allows you to support them in ways that are helpful, such as encouraging professional help, without enabling their behavior.

6. Protecting Yourself from Burnout

Loving an addict is emotionally exhausting. Daily. Letting go of the unrealistic expectation that you can "save" them protects you from burnout. Acceptance helps you recognize when it's time to take care of your own needs—physically, mentally, and emotionally.

7. Creating Space for the Addict's Growth

Ironically, by letting go, you may allow the addict to experience the consequences of their actions, which could motivate them to seek help. Often, the more we try to control or save someone, the more they resist. Acceptance creates space for the addict to take responsibility for their own recovery.

Letting go and acceptance are keys to your serenity. They also help to maintain your own health, protect the relationship from further damage, and allow the person struggling with addiction to own their journey.

What am I struggling to accept?

How would letting go of certain expectations change my emotional experience?

Write a letter of acceptance to yourself, acknowledging that the situation is beyond your control.

_____

_____

_____

_____

_____

_____

_____

_____

_____

_____

_____

_____

_____

_____

_____

_____

_____

Hope & Resilience

Hope and resilience are deeply intertwined with loving an addict, as they provide the emotional and psychological strength needed to navigate the complexities and challenges of addiction. Here's how both play an important role:

1. Hope Keeps You Going
When someone you love is struggling with addiction, hope is often what helps you hold on through difficult times. It fuels your belief that recovery is possible, even when the situation feels bleak. Hope helps prevent despair from taking over and provides a sense of possibility that things can improve, whether that means your loved one will find help or that you will find peace in the situation.

Hope for Recovery: Even in the darkest moments, believing in the potential for recovery can be crucial. Addiction is a disease, and like any disease, it can be treated. Hope keeps alive the idea that your loved one can overcome this and reclaim their life.

Hope for Change: It also represents the belief that relationships can heal, that progress is possible, and that even small steps toward recovery matter. Hope encourages patience and persistence in supporting the addict without losing sight of the potential for positive outcomes.

2. Resilience Helps You Endure

Resilience is the ability to bounce back and adapt, even in the face of prolonged hardship. Loving an addict can be an emotional rollercoaster, with ups and downs, relapses, and progress followed by setbacks. Resilience allows you to weather these storms without becoming completely overwhelmed or losing yourself in the process. And even though most days we want out of enduring our addicts, we still must endure on some level, regardless.

Emotional Strength: Resilience helps you stay emotionally stable, even when things feel chaotic. It enables you to recover from the emotional turmoil that often comes with addiction, such as disappointment, fear, or anger, and helps you maintain balance during crises.

Coping with Setbacks: Addiction is often marked by cycles of recovery and relapse. Resilience gives you the strength to face setbacks without losing hope or giving up. It enables you to handle the unpredictability and emotional toll that addiction will take on your soul.

Self-care and Boundaries: Resilience includes the ability to prioritize your own well-being, even while you love and support someone struggling with addiction. It allows you to set and maintain healthy boundaries, practice self-care, and prevent burnout or codependency.

4. Resilience Protects Against Emotional Exhaustion.
Being in a relationship with an addict is exhausting and draining, both mentally and emotionally. Resilience helps you recover from the emotional lows, allowing you to continue showing love and support without losing yourself. It protects against the emotional exhaustion that comes from repeated disappointments, broken promises, and setbacks.

5. Hope and Resilience in Balance
While hope provides optimism for the future, resilience grounds you in the reality that recovery is a long, difficult process. Balancing these two helps you remain compassionate and supportive without unrealistic expectations or being consumed by the addict's struggles. It allows you to support their journey while still taking care of your own mental and emotional health.

6. They Prevent Despair and Hopelessness
Without hope, it's easy to fall into despair, and without resilience, it's hard to handle the ongoing challenges of loving an addict. Together, they keep you from feeling stuck in helplessness and hopelessness. They give you the ability to face each new day with renewed strength, even when the path ahead is uncertain.

In essence, hope and resilience help you stay connected to your loved one while also protecting your own well-being. They allow you to offer support while still accepting that you cannot control their choices, and they help you maintain your emotional stability, no matter the outcome.

So far, how have I been resilient?

What small steps can I take to foster hope in the future?

Notes

Date

Support Network & Community

A solid support network is essential for someone who loves an addict. Why? Because it provides emotional strength, practical assistance, and a safe space for processing the complex emotions that come with the challenges of addiction. Here's why it matters:

1. Emotional Support and Validation

Loving an addict can feel isolating, as others may not fully understand the emotional rollercoaster involved. A support network, including friends, family, or a support group, provides a space where you can express your feelings without judgment. Being surrounded by people who understand or empathize helps you feel heard and validated, which is crucial for maintaining your emotional well-being.

Safe Space to Vent: You need a place to talk openly about your frustrations, fears, and heartache. Without this outlet, emotions can become overwhelming.

Preventing Emotional Burnout: Regularly leaning on a support network helps you manage stress and avoid emotional exhaustion, which is common when dealing with the unpredictable behaviors of addiction.

2. Perspective and Guidance

Support networks can offer perspective on what is healthy and realistic when you're deeply involved with an addict. They help you see beyond your immediate emotional reactions, offering advice or a fresh point of view that can guide you through difficult decisions. This is especially important when it comes to setting boundaries, which can be hard to maintain when you're emotionally invested.

Experienced Insight: People in support groups, like Al-Anon or Nar-Anon, often have been in similar situations and can share valuable insights on navigating life with an addicted loved one.

Clarity in Crisis: A support network helps you think more clearly during crises, offering guidance and advice to avoid impulsive decisions that might not serve your or the addict's best interest.

3. Practical Support

Loving someone with an addiction can be all-consuming, often requiring practical help in addition to emotional support. Friends, family, or even community organizations can step in to assist with daily life, providing everything from help with childcare to advice on navigating treatment options or financial challenges.

Assistance in Caregiving: A solid support system can help share the burden if you are taking care of the addict or managing the consequences of their behavior, like financial or legal issues.

Logistical Support: They can provide information about rehab programs, legal rights, or social services that might be useful as you navigate addiction and recovery options.

4. Encouragement to Set and Maintain Boundaries

One of the hardest aspects of loving an addict is learning to set healthy boundaries—knowing when to step in and when to step back. A strong support network helps you stay grounded in those boundaries by reminding you to take care of yourself, too. They can gently but firmly encourage you to hold firm when you are tempted to enable harmful behaviors or compromise your own well-being.

Accountability: A good support system keeps you accountable when you are tempted to break your own boundaries for the sake of the addict.

Empowering Healthy Choices: Supportive people remind you that it's okay—and necessary—to protect your emotional and mental health.

5. Reducing Isolation

Loving an addict is often as isolating experience, when others don't understand or stigmatize addiction. A support network helps you avoid feeling alone in your struggle, reminding you that you are not the only one going through this. It creates a sense of belonging and connection, which is vital for mental health.

Community of Shared Experience: Groups like Al-Anon or online communities bring together people with similar struggles, helping you realize that others share your feelings of frustration, sadness, or helplessness.

Social Interaction: Connecting with a support network also prevents withdrawal from social life, which can happen when you become overly focused on the addict's needs

.

6. Strength to Focus on Self-care

Support networks often act as reminders that your own well-being is just as important as your loved one's recovery. They encourage self-care practices, whether that's taking a break, seeking therapy, or simply allowing yourself the space to rest. They help prevent you from getting consumed by the addict's problems and neglecting your own needs.

Emotional and Mental Recharge: Self-care becomes more manageable with a network reminding you to step back when necessary.

Mental Health Resources: Supportive friends or professionals can recommend therapy, counseling, or coping strategies to help you manage your own emotional load.

7. Encouragement in Times of Doubt

Loving an addict often involves moments of doubt— wondering if you're doing the right thing, questioning your own decisions, or feeling uncertain about the future. A solid support network helps provide reassurance during those times, giving you the emotional boost you need to stay grounded and make thoughtful, balanced decisions.

Reinforcement of Strength: Support networks remind you that you are strong enough to get through the difficulties of loving an addict, especially during periods of relapse or struggle.

8. Breaking Codependency Patterns

Loving someone with an addiction can sometimes lead to codependency, where your identity becomes too wrapped up in the addict's life and choices. A support network can help you recognize and break these patterns by encouraging you to maintain independence and focus on your own goals, emotions, and life apart from the addict's struggles.

- **Promoting Individuality:** A solid support network helps you focus on your own needs and desires outside of the addict's recovery journey.
- **Preventing Self-sacrifice:** They remind you not to lose yourself in trying to save or control the addict's life, helping you maintain a healthier relationship dynamic.

A solid support network offers emotional, practical, and mental resilience, helping you maintain balance, and provides the strength while also protecting your own well-being.

Who can I turn to when things feel overwhelming?

_____
_____
_____
_____
_____
_____
_____
_____

How can I ask for help when I need it?

_____
_____
_____
_____
_____
_____
_____
_____

List of supportive people and resources

_____ _____
_____ _____
_____ _____
_____ _____
_____ _____
_____ _____
_____ _____

Notes

_____

_____

_____

_____

_____

_____

_____

_____

_____

_____

_____

_____

_____

_____

_____

_____

_____

_____

Quotes & Affirmations

Here are some powerful quotes and affirmations related to healing, strength, and perseverance. Use whichever ones feel real to you and write them down. Then, repeat them out loud daily. If you find other quotes and affirmations online, add them to your notes. It will help to retrain you brain to think positively. And when you think positively, you will feel positive! It takes approximately 21 days to form a new habit. So, start today! Why wait?

Healing

"Healing takes time, and asking for help is a courageous step."
– Mariska Hargitay

"Healing doesn't mean the damage never existed. It means the damage no longer controls our lives."
– Akshay Dubey

"You have the power to heal your life, and you need to know that."
– Louise Hay

"Healing is not linear, and it's okay to not be okay all the time."
-Anonymous

Affirmation: "I give myself permission to heal and move forward, one step at a time."

Strength

"You never know how strong you are until being strong is your only choice." – Bob Marley

"Strength grows in the moments when you think you can't go on but keep going anyway."
-Ed Mylett

"Out of suffering have emerged the strongest souls; the most massive characters are seared with scars." – Kahlil Gibran

"Do not pray for an easy life; pray for the strength to endure a difficult one."
– Bruce Lee

Affirmation: "I am stronger than I think, and I have the power to overcome any challenge."

Perseverance

"It always seems impossible until it's done."
– Nelson Mandela

"Perseverance is not a long race; it is many short races one after another."
– Walter Elliot

"Success is not final, failure is not fatal: It is the courage to continue that counts."
– Winston Churchill

"Fall seven times, stand up eight."
– Japanese Proverb

Affirmation: "I have the resilience and determination to keep moving forward, no matter how tough the journey gets."

Combination of Healing, Strength, & Perseverance

"The human capacity for burden is like bamboo— far more flexible than you'd ever believe at first glance." – Jodi Picoult

"The wound is the place where the Light enters you." – Rumi

"Scars are not signs of weakness, they are signs of survival and endurance."
– Rodney A. Winters

Affirmation: "I embrace my healing, trust my strength, and honor my perseverance through all of life's challenges."

Minfulness Practices

Here are some simple and effective mindfulness practices to help you stay grounded, reduce stress, and cultivate a sense of presence in your daily life. These exercises may be uncomfortable at first, especially when they are attempted in the midst of the latest drama your addicted loved one has created. But persevere. It will pay off. Promise.

1. Mindful Breathing
Focus on your breath to anchor yourself in the present moment. This practice can help calm your mind and reduce stress.

How to Practice: Sit or lie down in a comfortable position. Close your eyes and take a deep breath in through your nose for a count of four, hold for four, and exhale for four. Pay attention to the sensation of the breath entering and leaving your body. When your mind wanders, gently guide it back to your breathing.
Duration: 5–10 minutes.

2. Body Scan Meditation
A body scan is a way to bring awareness to different parts of your body and release physical tension.
How to Practice: Lie down in a quiet place. Close your eyes and focus on your breath for a minute. Then, slowly bring attention to different parts of your body, starting from your toes and working your way up to your head. Notice any sensations, tension, or discomfort, and consciously release tension as you move from one body part to the next.
Duration: 10–20 minutes.

3. Mindful Eating

This practice encourages you to slow down and fully experience your food, bringing awareness to the act of eating. It can open a whole new world for you. And it's fun.

How to Practice: Choose a meal or snack. Before you eat, take a moment to observe the food—its colors, textures, and smells. Eat slowly, paying attention to the taste, texture, and sensations of each bite. Chew thoroughly and notice the feeling of fullness. Avoid distractions like TV or phones while eating.
Duration: During a meal or snack.

4. Gratitude Practice

Practicing gratitude helps shift your focus from what's missing to what you already have. When in doubt, be grateful for something.

How to Practice: Each day, write down three things you're grateful for. They can be simple, like a warm bed, a conversation with a friend, or even the ability to breathe. Reflect on why you are thankful for each thing and how it positively affects your life.
Duration: 5 minutes daily.

5. Five Senses Exercise

This exercise is great for grounding yourself in the present moment, especially when you're feeling overwhelmed. And it can be fun.

How to Practice: Pause for a moment and focus on each of your five senses. Name:
5 things you can see,
4 things you can feel,
3 things you can hear,
2 things you can smell,
1 thing you can taste.
This brings your awareness back to the present and helps quiet your mind.
Duration: 5–10 minutes.

6. Walking Meditation

Walking meditation is a way to combine movement with mindfulness, which can be especially helpful for those who find it hard to sit still.

How to Practice: Find a quiet place to walk slowly. Focus on the sensation of your feet touching the ground, the movement of your legs, and the rhythm of your steps. Pay attention to your surroundings, including sounds, smells, and sights, but return your focus to your steps when your mind starts to wander.
Duration: 10–20 minutes.

7. Mindful Observation

This practice helps you reconnect with the beauty of your environment by focusing fully on a single object.

How to Practice: Choose an object in your environment, like a flower, tree, or even a cup of tea. Observe it closely for a few minutes. Notice its colors, shapes, textures, and how it interacts with light. The goal is to focus completely on the object, bringing your awareness to its details.
Duration: 3–5 minutes.

8. Loving-Kindness Meditation (Metta Meditation)

This practice involves cultivating compassion and love for yourself and others.

How to Practice: Sit quietly, close your eyes, and take a few deep breaths. Begin by silently repeating the following phrases: "May I be happy. May I be healthy. May I be safe. May I live with ease." After a few minutes, extend these wishes to others, such as loved ones, friends, or even difficult people in your life. You can say, "May you be happy. May you be healthy. May you be safe. May you live with ease."
Duration: 10–15 minutes.

9. Mindful Stretching or Yoga

Incorporating gentle stretching or yoga helps you connect with your body and breath while relieving tension.

How to Practice: Choose a few simple stretches or yoga poses. As you stretch, focus on your breath and the sensation in each muscle group. Move slowly and mindfully, paying attention to how your body feels during each movement.
Duration: 10–20 minutes.

10. Mindful Listening

This practice helps you develop a deeper sense of presence in your interactions with others.

How to Practice: The next time you are in conversation, focus entirely on what the other person is saying without planning your response or allowing your mind to wander. Notice their tone, body language, and words. By being fully present, you can engage more deeply and compassionately.
Duration: During conversations.

If none of these mindfulness practices appeal to you, the Internet is loaded with exercises that should. You have a whole world of information at your fingertips. Make it work for you!

Notes

Reflections on Growth

Looking back, in what ways have I grown?

_____

_____

_____

_____

_____

_____

_____

_____

_____

What plositive changes have come from this experience?

_____

_____

_____

_____

_____

_____

_____

_____

_____

_____

Notes

Notes

Day 2

What do I hope to gain from journaling through this experience?

_____

_____

_____

_____

_____

_____

_____

_____

_____

_____

_____

_____

_____

_____

_____

_____

_____

Set some self-care goals for yourself:

_____
_____
_____
_____
_____
_____
_____
_____
_____
_____
_____
_____
_____
_____
_____
_____
_____
_____
_____
_____

Date:

How am I feeling today: Happy Resentful Peaceful Sad Numb Furious Defeated Guilty Angry Depressed Empty Anxious Inspired Helpless Confused Held hostage Isolated

(Circle as many as are accurate)

Who or what triggered these emotions?

How did I react?

What emotions am I strugling with most now?

_____
_____
_____
_____
_____
_____
_____
_____
_____
_____
_____
_____
_____
_____

How has my child's addiction impacted me emotionally?

_____
_____
_____
_____
_____
_____
_____
_____
_____
_____
_____
_____
_____
_____
_____
_____
_____
_____

How can I handle it differently next time?

_____
_____
_____
_____
_____
_____
_____
_____
_____
_____
_____
_____
_____
_____

Notes

In what ways do I feel responsible for my loved one's addiction?

_____

_____

_____

_____

_____

_____

_____

_____

How can I startt to let go of feelings of guilt or blame?

_____

_____

_____

_____

_____

_____

_____

_____

I am full of compassion towards myself.
I release the stories that make me feel small.
I hold space for myself in this healing process.
I deserve happiness

Notes

What uncertainties am I coping with today?

_____

_____

_____

_____

_____

_____

What are the things within my control and what can I do about them?

_____

_____

_____

_____

_____

_____

_____

Refection Exercise

Write down both your fears and your hopes, then identify actionable steps to reduce the anxiety of uncertainties. i.e. yoga, exercise, refuse to answer the phone, etc.

What have I done for myself today?

It what ways can I promote more self-compassion?

Self –Care Check List

Circle as many as needed

Relaxing bath   Hobby   Write an email

Exercise   Relaxation techniques

Support group   Counseling   Movie

Journal writing   Walk   Day trip

Talk with a friend   Out to eat

Yoga   Read   Watch TV

Add more:

_____

_____

_____

by Noelle Rousseau

I wish someone would have told me that sacrificing my boundaries in the name of empathy wasn't noble .
I wish they would've warned me that all it would do is make me a safe house for other people's demons .
I think empathy has to be taught in two parts.
How to put yourself in someone else's shoes and see the hurt they were given that made them hurt you & how to understand that you still don't deserve what they're doing .
Their scars are no excuse for the wound they give to you .
Their inability to heal is not something you can fix .
If you give them excuses and safe places for their darkness instead of demanding they do better,
the only thing you are teaching them is that you will put up with it .
We want to live in a world where hurt people don't hurt people .
But the reality is, that starts with standing up for yourself and not accepting disrespect .
You choose to heal.
You choose to take the darkness the world gave you and still be the light.
You choose kindness despite the pain you received .

They can too.

What boundaries have I set for my loved one and how to I feel about them?

_____
_____
_____
_____
_____
_____
_____
_____
_____
_____

How do I respond when those boundaries are challenged?

_____
_____
_____
_____
_____
_____
_____
_____
_____
_____

Reflection:

Tips on maintaining boundaries

1. Clearly Define Your Boundaries

Take time to reflect on what behaviors you will and will not accept. Be specific and realistic about your limits. For example, you might set a boundary like, "I won't give you money, but I will help you find treatment options."

2. Communicate Boundaries Clearly

Once you've established your boundaries, communicate them to your loved one in a calm, direct, and compassionate manner. Make sure they understand what your limits are and what the consequences will be if those limits are crossed. You may have to write them down on paper to refer to if your loved one needs to be reminded. Texting those boundaries is also a good idea. These boundaries are not open for emotional negotiation.

3. Stay Consistent

This is a biggie, the linch pin on whether your boundary setting works or doesn't work. Consistency is key. If you waver on your boundaries, it sends mixed signals and may encourage manipulative behavior. Stick to your boundaries even if it's uncomfortable or your loved one pushes back.

4. Follow Through with Consequences

If your boundary is crossed, enforce the consequence you've communicated. For example, if you've said you won't lend money and they ask for it, remind them of your boundary and don't give in. DO NOT GIVE IN. Without consequences, boundaries lose their effectiveness.

5. Practice Self-Care

Maintaining boundaries with a loved one struggling with addiction is emotionally draining. Make sure you're taking care of yourself—whether it's through therapy, support groups, hobbies, or simply taking time for yourself to decompress. Healthy boundaries start with self-care. Repeat that. Healthy boundaries begin with self-care. Give yourself that much needed break from the chaos.

Notes

_____Date

_____

_____

_____

_____

_____

_____

_____

_____

_____

_____

_____

_____

_____

_____

_____

_____

_____

_____

_____

_____

_____

_____

Write 3 things you are grateful for:

1 _____

2 _____

3 _____

What lessons has this experience taught me about myself:

_____

_____

_____

_____

_____

_____

_____

_____

Who or what has been a source of support:

_____

_____

_____

Notes

_____ Date

What am I struggling to accept?

How would letting go of certain expectations change my emotional experience?

Write a letter of acceptance to yourself, acknowledging that the situation is beyond your control.

_____

_____

_____

_____

_____

_____

_____

_____

_____

_____

_____

_____

_____

_____

_____

_____

_____

_____

So far, how have I been resilient?

What small steps can I take to foster hope in the future?

Notes

Date
_____

Who can I turn to when things feel overwhelming?

_____
_____
_____
_____
_____
_____
_____
_____
_____

How can I ask for help when I need it?

_____
_____
_____
_____
_____
_____
_____
_____

List of supportive people and resources

_____ _____
_____ _____
_____ _____
_____ _____
_____ _____
_____ _____
_____ _____
_____ _____

Notes

_____

_____

_____

_____

_____

_____

_____

_____

_____

_____

_____

_____

_____

_____

_____

_____

_____

Quotes & Affirmations

Here are some powerful quotes and affirmations related to healing, strength, and perseverance. Use whichever ones feel real to you and write them down. Then, repeat them out loud daily. If you find other quotes and affirmations online, add them to your notes. It will help to retrain you brain to think positively. And when you think positively, you will feel positive! It takes approximately 21 days to form a new habit. So, start today! Why wait?

Healing

"Healing takes time, and asking for help is a courageous step."
– Mariska Hargitay

"Healing doesn't mean the damage never existed. It means the damage no longer controls our lives."
– Akshay Dubey

"You have the power to heal your life, and you need to know that."
– Louise Hay

"Healing is not linear, and it's okay to not be okay all the time."
-Anonymous

Affirmation: "I give myself permission to heal and move forward, one step at a time."

Strength

"You never know how strong you are until being strong is your only choice." – Bob Marley

"Strength grows in the moments when you think you can't go on but keep going anyway."
-Ed Mylett

"Out of suffering have emerged the strongest souls; the most massive characters are seared with scars." – Kahlil Gibran

"Do not pray for an easy life; pray for the strength to endure a difficult one."
– Bruce Lee

Affirmation: "I am stronger than I think, and I have the power to overcome any challenge."

Perseverance

"It always seems impossible until it's done."
– Nelson Mandela

"Perseverance is not a long race; it is many short races one after another."
– Walter Elliot

"Success is not final, failure is not fatal: It is the courage to continue that counts."
– Winston Churchill

"Fall seven times, stand up eight."
– Japanese Proverb

Affirmation: "I have the resilience and determination to keep moving forward, no matter how tough the journey gets."

Combination of Healing, Strength, & Perseverance

"The human capacity for burden is like bamboo—far more flexible than you'd ever believe at first glance." – Jodi Picoult

"The wound is the place where the Light enters you." – Rumi

"Scars are not signs of weakness, they are signs of survival and endurance."
– Rodney A. Winters

Affirmation: "I embrace my healing, trust my strength, and honor my perseverance through all of life's challenges."

.

Minfulness Practices

Here are some simple and effective mindfulness practices to help you stay grounded, reduce stress, and cultivate a sense of presence in your daily life. These exercises may be uncomfortable at first, especially when they are attempted in the midst of the latest drama your addicted loved one has created. But persevere. It will pay off. Promise.

1. Mindful Breathing
Focus on your breath to anchor yourself in the present moment. This practice can help calm your mind and reduce stress.

How to Practice: Sit or lie down in a comfortable position. Close your eyes and take a deep breath in through your nose for a count of four, hold for four, and exhale for four. Pay attention to the sensation of the breath entering and leaving your body. When your mind wanders, gently guide it back to your breathing.
Duration: 5–10 minutes.

2. Body Scan Meditation
A body scan is a way to bring awareness to different parts of your body and release physical tension.
How to Practice: Lie down in a quiet place. Close your eyes and focus on your breath for a minute. Then, slowly bring attention to different parts of your body, starting from your toes and working your way up to your head. Notice any sensations, tension, or discomfort, and consciously release tension as you move from one body part to the next.
Duration: 10–20 minutes.

3. Mindful Eating

This practice encourages you to slow down and fully experience your food, bringing awareness to the act of eating. It can open a whole new world for you. And it's fun.

How to Practice: Choose a meal or snack. Before you eat, take a moment to observe the food—its colors, textures, and smells. Eat slowly, paying attention to the taste, texture, and sensations of each bite. Chew thoroughly and notice the feeling of fullness. Avoid distractions like TV or phones while eating.
Duration: During a meal or snack.

4. Gratitude Practice

Practicing gratitude helps shift your focus from what's missing to what you already have. When in doubt, be grateful for something.

How to Practice: Each day, write down three things you're grateful for. They can be simple, like a warm bed, a conversation with a friend, or even the ability to breathe. Reflect on why you are thankful for each thing and how it positively affects your life.
Duration: 5 minutes daily.

5. Five Senses Exercise

This exercise is great for grounding yourself in the present moment, especially when you're feeling overwhelmed. And it can be fun.

How to Practice: Pause for a moment and focus on each of your five senses. Name:
5 things you can see,
4 things you can feel,
3 things you can hear,
2 things you can smell,
1 thing you can taste.
This brings your awareness back to the present and helps quiet your mind.
Duration: 5–10 minutes.

6. Walking Meditation

Walking meditation is a way to combine movement with mindfulness, which can be especially helpful for those who find it hard to sit still.

How to Practice: Find a quiet place to walk slowly. Focus on the sensation of your feet touching the ground, the movement of your legs, and the rhythm of your steps. Pay attention to your surroundings, including sounds, smells, and sights, but return your focus to your steps when your mind starts to wander.
Duration: 10–20 minutes.

7. Mindful Observation

This practice helps you reconnect with the beauty of your environment by focusing fully on a single object.

How to Practice: Choose an object in your environment, like a flower, tree, or even a cup of tea. Observe it closely for a few minutes. Notice its colors, shapes, textures, and how it interacts with light. The goal is to focus completely on the object, bringing your awareness to its details.
Duration: 3–5 minutes.

8. Loving-Kindness Meditation (Metta Meditation)

This practice involves cultivating compassion and love for yourself and others.

How to Practice: Sit quietly, close your eyes, and take a few deep breaths. Begin by silently repeating the following phrases: "May I be happy. May I be healthy. May I be safe. May I live with ease." After a few minutes, extend these wishes to others, such as loved ones, friends, or even difficult people in your life. You can say, "May you be happy. May you be healthy. May you be safe. May you live with ease."
Duration: 10–15 minutes.

9. Mindful Stretching or Yoga

Incorporating gentle stretching or yoga helps you connect with your body and breath while relieving tension.

How to Practice: Choose a few simple stretches or yoga poses. As you stretch, focus on your breath and the sensation in each muscle group. Move slowly and mindfully, paying attention to how your body feels during each movement.
Duration: 10–20 minutes.

10. Mindful Listening

This practice helps you develop a deeper sense of presence in your interactions with others.

How to Practice: The next time you are in conversation, focus entirely on what the other person is saying without planning your response or allowing your mind to wander. Notice their tone, body language, and words. By being fully present, you can engage more deeply and compassionately.
Duration: During conversations.

If none of these mindfulness practices appeal to you, the Internet is loaded with exercises that should. You have a whole world of information at your fingertips. Make it work for you!

Notes

Reflections on Growth

Looking back, in what ways have I grown?

_____

_____

_____

_____

_____

_____

_____

_____

_____

What plositive changes have come from this experience?

_____

_____

_____

_____

_____

_____

_____

_____

_____

_____

_____

Notes

Day 3

What do I hope to gain from journaling through this experience?

_____
_____
_____
_____
_____
_____
_____
_____
_____
_____
_____
_____
_____
_____
_____
_____
_____
_____
_____
_____

Set some self-care goals for yourself:

Date:

How am I feeling today: Happy Resentful Peaceful Sad Numb

Furious Defeated Guilty Angry Depressed Empty Anxious

Inspired Helpless Confused Held hostage Isolated

(Circle as many as are accurate)

Who or what triggered these emotions?

How did I react?

What emotions am I strugling with most now?

How has my child's addiction impacted me emotionally?

_____
_____
_____
_____
_____
_____
_____
_____
_____
_____
_____
_____
_____
_____
_____

How can I handle it differently next time?

_____
_____
_____
_____
_____
_____
_____
_____
_____
_____
_____
_____
_____
_____

Notes

In what ways do I feel responsible for my loved one's addiction?

_____

_____

_____

_____

_____

_____

_____

_____

How can I startt to let go of feelings of guilt or blame?

_____

_____

_____

_____

_____

_____

_____

_____

I am full of compassion towards myself.
I release the stories that make me feel small.
I hold space for myself in this healing process.
I deserve happiness

Notes

What uncertainties am I coping with today?

What are the things within my control and what can I do about them?

Refection Exercise

Write down both your fears and your hopes, then identify actionable steps to reduce the anxiety of uncertainties. i.e. yoga, exercise, refuse to answer the phone, etc.

What have I done for myself today?

_____

_____

_____

_____

_____

It what ways can I promote more self-compassion?

_____

_____

_____

_____

_____

_____

Self −Care Check List

Circle as many as needed

Relaxing bath   Hobby   Write an email

Exercise   Relaxation techniques

Support group   Counseling   Movie

Journal writing   Walk   Day trip

Talk with a friend   Out to eat

Yoga   Read   Watch TV

Add more:

_____

_____

_____

by Noelle Rousseau

I wish someone would have told me that sacrificing my boundaries in the name of empathy wasn't noble .
I wish they would've warned me that all it would do is make me a safe house for other people's demons .
I think empathy has to be taught in two parts.
How to put yourself in someone else's shoes and see the hurt they were given that made them hurt you & how to understand that you still don't deserve what they're doing .
Their scars are no excuse for the wound they give to you .
Their inability to heal is not something you can fix .
If you give them excuses and safe places for their darkness instead of demanding they do better,
the only thing you are teaching them is that you will put up with it .
We want to live in a world where hurt people don't hurt people .
But the reality is, that starts with standing up for yourself and not accepting disrespect .
You choose to heal.
You choose to take the darkness the world gave you and still be the light.
You choose kindness despite the pain you received .

They can too.

What boundaries have I set for my loved one and how to I feel about them?

_____

_____

_____

_____

_____

_____

_____

_____

_____

How do I respond when those boundaries are challenged?

_____

_____

_____

_____

_____

_____

_____

_____

_____

Reflection:

Tips on maintaining boundaries

1. Clearly Define Your Boundaries
Take time to reflect on what behaviors you will and will not accept. Be specific and realistic about your limits. For example, you might set a boundary like, "I won't give you money, but I will help you find treatment options."

2. Communicate Boundaries Clearly
Once you've established your boundaries, communicate them to your loved one in a calm, direct, and compassionate manner. Make sure they understand what your limits are and what the consequences will be if those limits are crossed. You may have to write them down on paper to refer to if your loved one needs to be reminded. Texting those boundaries is also a good idea. These boundaries are not open for emotional negotiation.

3. Stay Consistent
This is a biggie, the linch pin on whether your boundary setting works or doesn't work. Consistency is key. If you waver on your boundaries, it sends mixed signals and may encourage manipulative behavior. Stick to your boundaries even if it's uncomfortable or your loved one pushes back.

4. Follow Through with Consequences

If your boundary is crossed, enforce the consequence you've communicated. For example, if you've said you won't lend money and they ask for it, remind them of your boundary and don't give in. DO NOT GIVE IN. Without consequences, boundaries lose their effectiveness.

5. Practice Self-Care

Maintaining boundaries with a loved one struggling with addiction is emotionally draining. Make sure you're taking care of yourself—whether it's through therapy, support groups, hobbies, or simply taking time for yourself to decompress. Healthy boundaries start with self-care. Repeat that. Healthy boundaries begin with self-care. Give yourself that much needed break from the chaos.

Notes

_____Date

Write 3 things you are grateful for:

1 _____

2 _____

3 _____

What lessons has this experience taught me about myself:

_____

_____

_____

_____

_____

_____

_____

_____

_____

Who or what has been a source of support:

_____

_____

_____

_____

Notes

Date _____

What am I struggling to accept?

How would letting go of certain expectations change my emotional experience?

Write a letter of acceptance to yourself, acknowledging that the situation is beyond your control.

_____

_____

_____

_____

_____

_____

_____

_____

_____

_____

_____

_____

_____

_____

_____

_____

So far, how have I been resilient?

What small steps can I take to foster hope in the future?

Notes

Date _____

Who can I turn to when things feel overwhelming?

_____
_____
_____
_____
_____
_____
_____
_____

How can I ask for help when I need it?

_____
_____
_____
_____
_____
_____
_____
_____

List of supportive people and resources

_____ _____
_____ _____
_____ _____
_____ _____
_____ _____
_____ _____
_____ _____
_____ _____

Notes

Quotes & Affirmations

Here are some powerful quotes and affirmations related to healing, strength, and perseverance. Use whichever ones feel real to you and write them down. Then, repeat them out loud daily. If you find other quotes and affirmations online, add them to your notes. It will help to retrain you brain to think positively. And when you think positively, you will feel positive! It takes approximately 21 days to form a new habit. So, start today! Why wait?

Healing

"Healing takes time, and asking for help is a courageous step."
– Mariska Hargitay

"Healing doesn't mean the damage never existed. It means the damage no longer controls our lives."
– Akshay Dubey

"You have the power to heal your life, and you need to know that."
– Louise Hay

"Healing is not linear, and it's okay to not be okay all the time."
-Anonymous

Affirmation: "I give myself permission to heal and move forward, one step at a time."

Strength

"You never know how strong you are until being strong is your only choice." – Bob Marley

"Strength grows in the moments when you think you can't go on but keep going anyway."
-Ed Mylett

"Out of suffering have emerged the strongest souls; the most massive characters are seared with scars." – Kahlil Gibran

"Do not pray for an easy life; pray for the strength to endure a difficult one."
– Bruce Lee

Affirmation: "I am stronger than I think, and I have the power to overcome any challenge."

Perseverance

"It always seems impossible until it's done."
– Nelson Mandela

"Perseverance is not a long race; it is many short races one after another."
– Walter Elliot

"Success is not final, failure is not fatal: It is the courage to continue that counts."
– Winston Churchill

"Fall seven times, stand up eight."
– Japanese Proverb

Affirmation: "I have the resilience and determination to keep moving forward, no matter how tough the journey gets."

Combination of Healing, Strength, & Perseverance

"The human capacity for burden is like bamboo— far more flexible than you'd ever believe at first glance." – Jodi Picoult

"The wound is the place where the Light enters you." – Rumi

"Scars are not signs of weakness, they are signs of survival and endurance."
– Rodney A. Winters

Affirmation: "I embrace my healing, trust my strength, and honor my perseverance through all of life's challenges."

Minfulness Practices

Here are some simple and effective mindfulness practices to help you stay grounded, reduce stress, and cultivate a sense of presence in your daily life. These exercises may be uncomfortable at first, especially when they are attempted in the midst of the latest drama your addicted loved one has created. But persevere. It will pay off. Promise.

1. Mindful Breathing
Focus on your breath to anchor yourself in the present moment. This practice can help calm your mind and reduce stress.

How to Practice: Sit or lie down in a comfortable position. Close your eyes and take a deep breath in through your nose for a count of four, hold for four, and exhale for four. Pay attention to the sensation of the breath entering and leaving your body. When your mind wanders, gently guide it back to your breathing.
Duration: 5–10 minutes.

2. Body Scan Meditation
A body scan is a way to bring awareness to different parts of your body and release physical tension.
How to Practice: Lie down in a quiet place. Close your eyes and focus on your breath for a minute. Then, slowly bring attention to different parts of your body, starting from your toes and working your way up to your head. Notice any sensations, tension, or discomfort, and consciously release tension as you move from one body part to the next.
Duration: 10–20 minutes.

3. Mindful Eating

This practice encourages you to slow down and fully experience your food, bringing awareness to the act of eating. It can open a whole new world for you. And it's fun.

How to Practice: Choose a meal or snack. Before you eat, take a moment to observe the food—its colors, textures, and smells. Eat slowly, paying attention to the taste, texture, and sensations of each bite. Chew thoroughly and notice the feeling of fullness. Avoid distractions like TV or phones while eating.
Duration: During a meal or snack.

4. Gratitude Practice

Practicing gratitude helps shift your focus from what's missing to what you already have. When in doubt, be grateful for something.

How to Practice: Each day, write down three things you're grateful for. They can be simple, like a warm bed, a conversation with a friend, or even the ability to breathe. Reflect on why you are thankful for each thing and how it positively affects your life.
Duration: 5 minutes daily.

5. Five Senses Exercise

This exercise is great for grounding yourself in the present moment, especially when you're feeling overwhelmed. And it can be fun.

How to Practice: Pause for a moment and focus on each of your five senses. Name:
5 things you can see,
4 things you can feel,
3 things you can hear,
2 things you can smell,
1 thing you can taste.
This brings your awareness back to the present and helps quiet your mind.
Duration: 5–10 minutes.

6. Walking Meditation

Walking meditation is a way to combine movement with mindfulness, which can be especially helpful for those who find it hard to sit still.

How to Practice: Find a quiet place to walk slowly. Focus on the sensation of your feet touching the ground, the movement of your legs, and the rhythm of your steps. Pay attention to your surroundings, including sounds, smells, and sights, but return your focus to your steps when your mind starts to wander.
Duration: 10–20 minutes.

7. Mindful Observation

This practice helps you reconnect with the beauty of your environment by focusing fully on a single object.

How to Practice: Choose an object in your environment, like a flower, tree, or even a cup of tea. Observe it closely for a few minutes. Notice its colors, shapes, textures, and how it interacts with light. The goal is to focus completely on the object, bringing your awareness to its details.
Duration: 3–5 minutes.

8. Loving-Kindness Meditation (Metta Meditation)

This practice involves cultivating compassion and love for yourself and others.

How to Practice: Sit quietly, close your eyes, and take a few deep breaths. Begin by silently repeating the following phrases: "May I be happy. May I be healthy. May I be safe. May I live with ease." After a few minutes, extend these wishes to others, such as loved ones, friends, or even difficult people in your life. You can say, "May you be happy. May you be healthy. May you be safe. May you live with ease."
Duration: 10–15 minutes.

9. Mindful Stretching or Yoga

Incorporating gentle stretching or yoga helps you connect with your body and breath while relieving tension.

How to Practice: Choose a few simple stretches or yoga poses. As you stretch, focus on your breath and the sensation in each muscle group. Move slowly and mindfully, paying attention to how your body feels during each movement.
Duration: 10–20 minutes.

10. Mindful Listening

This practice helps you develop a deeper sense of presence in your interactions with others.

How to Practice: The next time you are in conversation, focus entirely on what the other person is saying without planning your response or allowing your mind to wander. Notice their tone, body language, and words. By being fully present, you can engage more deeply and compassionately.
Duration: During conversations.

If none of these mindfulness practices appeal to you, the Internet is loaded with exercises that should. You have a whole world of information at your fingertips. Make it work for you!

Notes

Reflections on Growth

Looking back, in what ways have I grown?

_____

_____

_____

_____

_____

_____

_____

_____

_____

What plositive changes have come from this experience?

_____

_____

_____

_____

_____

_____

_____

_____

_____

Notes

Day 4

What do I hope to gain from journaling through this experience?

_____
_____
_____
_____
_____
_____
_____
_____
_____
_____
_____
_____
_____
_____
_____
_____
_____

Set some self-care goals for yourself:

Date:

How am I feeling today: Happy Resentful Peaceful Sad Numb

Furious Defeated Guilty Angry Depressed Empty Anxious

Inspired Helpless Confused Held hostage Isolated

(Circle as many as are accurate)

Who or what triggered these emotions?

How did I react?

What emotions am I strugling with most now?

How has my child's addiction impacted me emotionally?

_____
_____
_____
_____
_____
_____
_____
_____
_____
_____
_____
_____
_____
_____
_____
_____

How can I handle it differently next time?

_____
_____
_____
_____
_____
_____
_____
_____
_____
_____
_____
_____

Notes

In what ways do I feel responsible for my loved one's addiction?

_____

_____

_____

_____

_____

_____

_____

How can I startt to let go of feelings of guilt or blame?

_____

_____

_____

_____

_____

_____

_____

_____

I am full of compassion towards myself.
I release the stories that make me feel small.
I hold space for myself in this healing process.
I deserve happiness

Notes

What uncertainties am I coping with today?

_____
_____
_____
_____
_____
_____

What are the things within my control and what can I do about them?

_____
_____
_____
_____
_____
_____
_____

Refection Exercise

Write down both your fears and your hopes, then identify actionable steps to reduce the anxiety of uncertainties. i.e. yoga, exercise, refuse to answer the phone, etc.

_____

_____

_____

_____

_____

_____

_____

_____

_____

_____

_____

_____

_____

_____

What have I done for myself today?

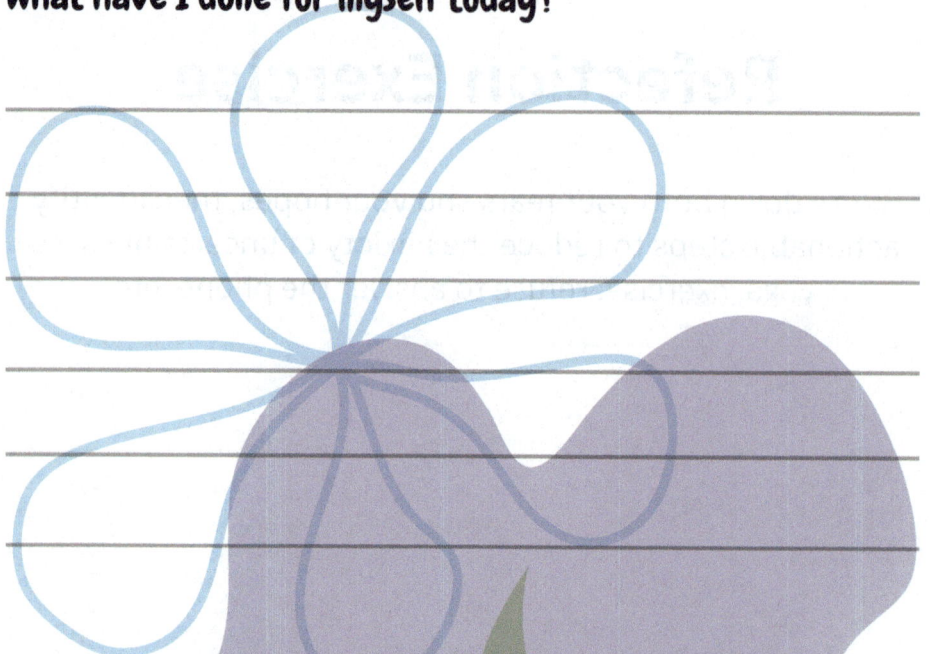

It what ways can I promote more self-compassion?

Self –Care Check List

Circle as many as needed

Relaxing bath   Hobby   Write an email

Exercise   Relaxation techniques

Support group   Counseling   Movie

Journal writing   Walk   Day trip

Talk with a friend   Out to eat

Yoga   Read   Watch TV

Add more:

_____

_____

_____

by Noelle Rousseau

I wish someone would have told me that sacrificing my boundaries in the name of empathy wasn't noble .
I wish they would've warned me that all it would do is make me a safe house for other people's demons .
I think empathy has to be taught in two parts.
How to put yourself in someone else's shoes and see the hurt they were given that made them hurt you & how to understand that you still don't deserve what they're doing .
Their scars are no excuse for the wound they give to you .
Their inability to heal is not something you can fix .
If you give them excuses and safe places for their darkness instead of demanding they do better,
the only thing you are teaching them is that you will put up with it .
We want to live in a world where hurt people don't hurt people .
But the reality is, that starts with standing up for yourself and not accepting disrespect .
You choose to heal.
You choose to take the darkness the world gave you and still be the light.
You choose kindness despite the pain you received .

They can too.

What boundaries have I set for my loved one and how to I feel about them?

_____
_____
_____
_____
_____
_____
_____
_____

How do I respond when those boundaries are challenged?

_____
_____
_____
_____
_____
_____
_____
_____

Reflection:

Tips on maintaining boundaries

1. Clearly Define Your Boundaries

Take time to reflect on what behaviors you will and will not accept. Be specific and realistic about your limits. For example, you might set a boundary like, "I won't give you money, but I will help you find treatment options."

2. Communicate Boundaries Clearly

Once you've established your boundaries, communicate them to your loved one in a calm, direct, and compassionate manner. Make sure they understand what your limits are and what the consequences will be if those limits are crossed. You may have to write them down on paper to refer to if your loved one needs to be reminded. Texting those boundaries is also a good idea. These boundaries are not open for emotional negotiation.

3. Stay Consistent

This is a biggie, the linch pin on whether your boundary setting works or doesn't work. Consistency is key. If you waver on your boundaries, it sends mixed signals and may encourage manipulative behavior. Stick to your boundaries even if it's uncomfortable or your loved one pushes back.

4. Follow Through with Consequences
If your boundary is crossed, enforce the consequence you've communicated. For example, if you've said you won't lend money and they ask for it, remind them of your boundary and don't give in. DO NOT GIVE IN. Without consequences, boundaries lose their effectiveness.

5. Practice Self-Care
Maintaining boundaries with a loved one struggling with addiction is emotionally draining. Make sure you're taking care of yourself—whether it's through therapy, support groups, hobbies, or simply taking time for yourself to decompress. Healthy boundaries start with self-care. Repeat that. Healthy boundaries begin with self-care. Give yourself that much needed break from the chaos.

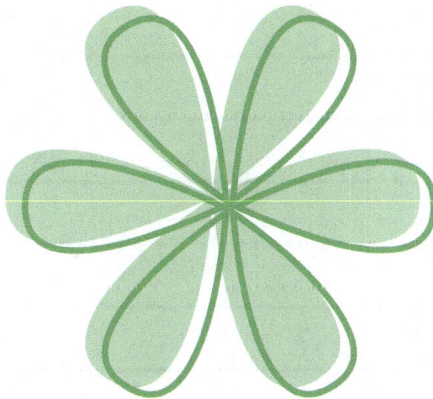

Notes

_____Date

_____

_____

_____

_____

_____

_____

_____

_____

_____

_____

_____

_____

_____

_____

_____

_____

_____

_____

_____

Write 3 things you are grateful for:

1

2

3

What lessons has this experience taught me about myself:

Who or what has been a source of support:

Notes

Date _____

What am I struggling to accept?

How would letting go of certain expectations change my emotional experience?

Write a letter of acceptance to yourself, acknowledging that the situation is beyond your control.

_____

_____

_____

_____

_____

_____

_____

_____

_____

_____

_____

_____

_____

_____

_____

_____

So far, how have I been resilient?

What small steps can I take to foster hope in the future?

Notes

Date
_____

Who can I turn to when things feel overwhelming?

_____
_____
_____
_____
_____
_____
_____
_____

How can I ask for help when I need it?

_____
_____
_____
_____
_____
_____
_____
_____

List of supportive people and resources

_____   _____
_____   _____
_____   _____
_____   _____
_____   _____
_____   _____
_____   _____

Notes

_____

_____

_____

_____

_____

_____

_____

_____

_____

_____

_____

_____

_____

_____

_____

_____

Quotes & Affirmations

Here are some powerful quotes and affirmations related to healing, strength, and perseverance. Use whichever ones feel real to you and write them down. Then, repeat them out loud daily. If you find other quotes and affirmations online, add them to your notes. It will help to retrain you brain to think positively. And when you think positively, you will feel positive! It takes approximately 21 days to form a new habit. So, start today! Why wait?

Healing

"Healing takes time, and asking for help is a courageous step."
– Mariska Hargitay

"Healing doesn't mean the damage never existed. It means the damage no longer controls our lives."
– Akshay Dubey

"You have the power to heal your life, and you need to know that."
– Louise Hay

"Healing is not linear, and it's okay to not be okay all the time."
-Anonymous

Affirmation: "I give myself permission to heal and move forward, one step at a time."

Strength

"You never know how strong you are until being strong is your only choice." – Bob Marley

"Strength grows in the moments when you think you can't go on but keep going anyway."
-Ed Mylett

"Out of suffering have emerged the strongest souls; the most massive characters are seared with scars." – Kahlil Gibran

"Do not pray for an easy life; pray for the strength to endure a difficult one."
– Bruce Lee

Affirmation: "I am stronger than I think, and I have the power to overcome any challenge."

Perseverance

"It always seems impossible until it's done."
– Nelson Mandela

"Perseverance is not a long race; it is many short races one after another."
– Walter Elliot

"Success is not final, failure is not fatal: It is the courage to continue that counts."
– Winston Churchill

"Fall seven times, stand up eight."
– Japanese Proverb

Affirmation: "I have the resilience and determination to keep moving forward, no matter how tough the journey gets."

Combination of Healing, Strength, & Perseverance

"The human capacity for burden is like bamboo—far more flexible than you'd ever believe at first glance." – Jodi Picoult

"The wound is the place where the Light enters you." – Rumi

"Scars are not signs of weakness, they are signs of survival and endurance."
– Rodney A. Winters

Affirmation: "I embrace my healing, trust my strength, and honor my perseverance through all of life's challenges."

Minfulness Practices

Here are some simple and effective mindfulness practices to help you stay grounded, reduce stress, and cultivate a sense of presence in your daily life. These exercises may be uncomfortable at first, especially when they are attempted in the midst of the latest drama your addicted loved one has created. But persevere. It will pay off. Promise.

1. Mindful Breathing
Focus on your breath to anchor yourself in the present moment. This practice can help calm your mind and reduce stress.

How to Practice: Sit or lie down in a comfortable position. Close your eyes and take a deep breath in through your nose for a count of four, hold for four, and exhale for four. Pay attention to the sensation of the breath entering and leaving your body. When your mind wanders, gently guide it back to your breathing.
Duration: 5–10 minutes.

2. Body Scan Meditation
A body scan is a way to bring awareness to different parts of your body and release physical tension.
How to Practice: Lie down in a quiet place. Close your eyes and focus on your breath for a minute. Then, slowly bring attention to different parts of your body, starting from your toes and working your way up to your head. Notice any sensations, tension, or discomfort, and consciously release tension as you move from one body part to the next.
Duration: 10–20 minutes.

3. Mindful Eating

This practice encourages you to slow down and fully experience your food, bringing awareness to the act of eating. It can open a whole new world for you. And it's fun.

How to Practice: Choose a meal or snack. Before you eat, take a moment to observe the food—its colors, textures, and smells. Eat slowly, paying attention to the taste, texture, and sensations of each bite. Chew thoroughly and notice the feeling of fullness. Avoid distractions like TV or phones while eating.
Duration: During a meal or snack.

4. Gratitude Practice

Practicing gratitude helps shift your focus from what's missing to what you already have. When in doubt, be grateful for something.

How to Practice: Each day, write down three things you're grateful for. They can be simple, like a warm bed, a conversation with a friend, or even the ability to breathe. Reflect on why you are thankful for each thing and how it positively affects your life.
Duration: 5 minutes daily.

5. Five Senses Exercise

This exercise is great for grounding yourself in the present moment, especially when you're feeling overwhelmed. And it can be fun.

How to Practice: Pause for a moment and focus on each of your five senses. Name:
5 things you can see,
4 things you can feel,
3 things you can hear,
2 things you can smell,
1 thing you can taste.
This brings your awareness back to the present and helps quiet your mind.
Duration: 5–10 minutes.

6. Walking Meditation

Walking meditation is a way to combine movement with mindfulness, which can be especially helpful for those who find it hard to sit still.

How to Practice: Find a quiet place to walk slowly. Focus on the sensation of your feet touching the ground, the movement of your legs, and the rhythm of your steps. Pay attention to your surroundings, including sounds, smells, and sights, but return your focus to your steps when your mind starts to wander.
Duration: 10–20 minutes.

7. Mindful Observation

This practice helps you reconnect with the beauty of your environment by focusing fully on a single object.

How to Practice: Choose an object in your environment, like a flower, tree, or even a cup of tea. Observe it closely for a few minutes. Notice its colors, shapes, textures, and how it interacts with light. The goal is to focus completely on the object, bringing your awareness to its details.
Duration: 3–5 minutes.

8. Loving-Kindness Meditation (Metta Meditation)

This practice involves cultivating compassion and love for yourself and others.

How to Practice: Sit quietly, close your eyes, and take a few deep breaths. Begin by silently repeating the following phrases: "May I be happy. May I be healthy. May I be safe. May I live with ease." After a few minutes, extend these wishes to others, such as loved ones, friends, or even difficult people in your life. You can say, "May you be happy. May you be healthy. May you be safe. May you live with ease."
Duration: 10–15 minutes.

9. Mindful Stretching or Yoga

Incorporating gentle stretching or yoga helps you connect with your body and breath while relieving tension.

How to Practice: Choose a few simple stretches or yoga poses. As you stretch, focus on your breath and the sensation in each muscle group. Move slowly and mindfully, paying attention to how your body feels during each movement.
Duration: 10–20 minutes.

10. Mindful Listening

This practice helps you develop a deeper sense of presence in your interactions with others.

How to Practice: The next time you are in conversation, focus entirely on what the other person is saying without planning your response or allowing your mind to wander. Notice their tone, body language, and words. By being fully present, you can engage more deeply and compassionately.
Duration: During conversations.

If none of these mindfulness practices appeal to you, the Internet is loaded with exercises that should. You have a whole world of information at your fingertips. Make it work for you!

Notes

Reflections on Growth

Looking back, in what ways have I grown?

_____

_____

_____

_____

_____

_____

_____

_____

What plositive changes have come from this experience?

_____

_____

_____

_____

_____

_____

_____

_____

_____

Day 5

What do I hope to gain from journaling through this experience?

Set some self-care goals for yourself:

_____
_____
_____
_____
_____
_____
_____
_____
_____
_____
_____
_____
_____
_____
_____
_____
_____
_____

Date:

How am I feeling today: Happy Resentful Peaceful Sad Numb Furious Defeated Guilty Angry Depressed Empty Anxious Inspired Helpless Confused Held hostage Isolated

(Circle as many as are accurate)

Who or what triggered these emotions?

How did I react?

What emotions am I strugling with most now?

How has my child's addiction impacted me emotionally?

_____
_____
_____
_____
_____
_____
_____
_____
_____
_____
_____
_____
_____
_____
_____

How can I handle it differently next time?

_____
_____
_____
_____
_____
_____
_____
_____
_____
_____
_____
_____
_____

Notes

Managing Guilt & Shame

Managing guilt and shame when dealing with an addicted loved one can be incredibly challenging. These emotions are natural, but they can be overwhelming and detrimental to your mental health. Acknowledge and validate your emotions. This journal will help you accomplish this.

Accept that your feelings are normal because they are! You'd have to be crazy to tolerate some of the situations the addict creates. Remember that guilt and shame are common reactions when someone you care about is struggling with addiction, so it's important to validate that these feelings are part of the process.

Trying to ignore or bury guilt and shame will often intensify them. Find a healthy outlet, like this journal, or by talking to a therapist, or confiding in a trusted friend is essential.

Realize that addiction is a disease: Addiction is a complex condition, not a moral failing. Your loved one's addiction is not your fault, and understanding the science behind addiction can help alleviate feelings of guilt.

Separate the person from the addiction: Recognize that your loved one's actions while in addiction are influenced by their illness, and not a reflection of their true self.

◇ ◇ ◇

Remember, you are not responsible for "fixing" your loved one. Setting limits helps protect your own mental and emotional well-being. It can be difficult to say no, but healthy boundaries prevent you from being consumed by guilt. DON'T FEEL GUILTY ABOUT SETTING BOUNDARIES!

While you can offer support, focus on healing yourself. The path to recovery, for **both** you and your loved one, is a process that takes time, patience, and self-compassion.

Release the burden of guilt by practicing self-forgiveness. You cannot go back and change the past, but you can choose to move forward with more knowledge and compassion. This doesn't mean condoning harmful behavior, but letting go of resentment about it can free you from emotional pain.

Participate more fully on your own life. Your life needs more of YOU, and less of the addict.

In what ways do I feel responsible for my loved one's addiction?

_____

_____

_____

_____

_____

_____

_____

_____

How can I startt to let go of feelings of guilt or blame?

_____

_____

_____

_____

_____

_____

_____

_____

_____

I am full of compassion towards myself.
I release the stories that make me feel small.
I hold space for myself in this healing process.
I deserve happiness

Notes

_____
_____
_____
_____
_____
_____
_____
_____
_____
_____
_____
_____
_____
_____
_____
_____
_____
_____
_____
_____
_____
_____
_____
_____

Coping with Uncertainty

Uncertainty is the only thing we can be certain about when dealing with an addicted loved one. Their moods can change from one minute to the next and so can their irresponsible decisions. You may never be sure how the person will react in certain situations or whether they will keep promises.

Trust is often damaged by the dishonesty, manipulation, or betrayal that can accompany addiction. Rebuilding trust can be uncertain and takes time, and you may wonder if the person will ever be truthful or reliable again.

Addiction can lead to financial instability for the person suffering and for those around them. There can be uncertainties around how much support to offer, whether it will be misused, or if financial losses will affect long-term stability.

The future of someone battling addiction is often unclear. You may worry about their health, well-being, and ability to recover in the long term chronic effects. Will today be the day you get 'the call'?

Depending on the addiction, legal problems or dangerous situations can be highly unpredictable, whether it's related to illegal substances, DUIs, or other risky behaviors.

Then there is the uncertainty of answering the phone whenever it rings! Will they ask for money again? Be verbally abusive again? Threaten you again?

What uncertainties am I coping with today?

_____

_____

_____

_____

_____

_____

What are the things within my control and what can I do about them?

_____

_____

_____

_____

_____

_____

_____

Refection Exercise

Write down both your fears and your hopes, then identify actionable steps to reduce the anxiety of uncertainties. i.e. yoga, exercise, refuse to answer the phone, etc.

Practicing Self-Compassion & Self-Care
What about YOU?

Loving someone with an addiction can be so incredibly challenging, that we forget about our own needs in favor of the addict's demands and inconsistencies. Therefore, it's twice as important and twice as difficult, to prioritize self-compassion and self-care. But our emotional lives depend upon it. Here are some helpful ways to love yourself:

- **Establish clear boundaries to prevent the addict's behavior from overwhelming your life**. Boundaries might involve limiting financial support, maintaining emotional distance when necessary, or refusing to engage in conversations when the person is under the influence.

- **Be kind to yourself in moments of emotional struggle**. Speak to yourself as you would to a friend in a similar situation, with understanding and care.

- **It can be helpful to have people who can listen without judgment.** Join Support Groups: Consider groups like Al-Anon or Nar-Anon, where you can connect with others who understand the complexities of loving someone with an addiction.

- **Engage in activities that nourish your mind, body, and spirit.** Whether it's exercise, meditation, journaling, or hobbies, self-care isn't selfish; it's necessary.

- **Maintain Routines:** Structure and routine can help you feel grounded. Continue focusing on your own goals and daily activities, even when the addict's behavior feels all-consuming.

- **Detach with love**. Detaching with love means caring for the person without feeling responsible for their choices or enabling their addiction. You can offer support, but their recovery is ultimately their responsibility.

- **Acknowledge your efforts.** Recognize the strength it takes to love someone with an addiction, and be proud of the steps you've taken to care for yourself. Celebrate small victories in maintaining your boundaries and emotional health.

No one is going to take care of you, but you! It sure won't be your addicted loved one. Keep this foremost in your mind, not as a source of resentment toward them but as a simple reality that needs to be honored.

What have I done for myself today?

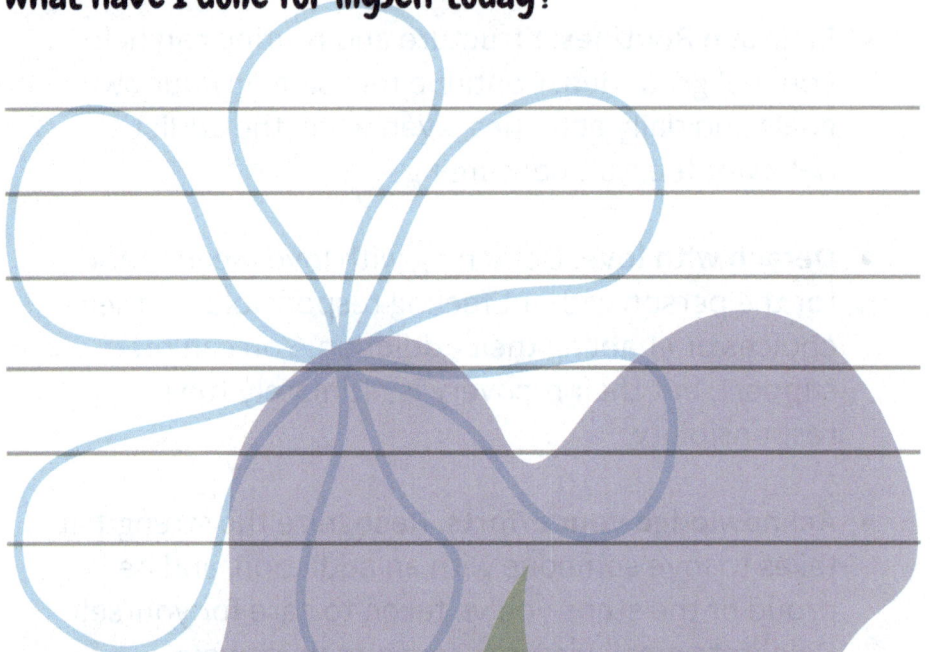

_____

_____

_____

_____

_____

_____

It what ways can I promote more self-compassion?

_____

_____

_____

_____

_____

_____

_____

_____

Self –Care Check List

Circle as many as needed

Relaxing bath   Hobby   Write an email

Exercise   Relaxation techniques

Support group   Counseling   Movie

Journal writing   Walk   Day trip

Talk with a friend   Out to eat

Yoga   Read   Watch TV

Add more:

_____

_____

_____

Setting Boundaries

Setting boundaries with addicted loved ones is crucial for several reasons, both for your well-being and theirs. Without boundaires, we are held hostage to someone else's addiction. We are stuck in their addiction with them. Here's why setting clear boundaries is important:

1. Protects Your Emotional and Mental Health
Addiction can create emotional chaos, leading to stress, anxiety, and burnout for family members and friends. Boundaries help maintain your mental health by giving you control over what behavior you will and will not tolerate. It allows you to keep a healthier emotional distance from destructive patterns.

2. Promotes Personal Accountability
By setting boundaries, you encourage the addicted person to take responsibility for their actions. If they experience the natural consequences of their behavior, they are more likely to realize the need for change. Enabling, on the other hand, can perpetuate the addiction.

3. Prevents Codependency
Without boundaries, there is a risk of falling into a codependent relationship where you prioritize their needs over your own. This dynamic can reinforce unhealthy behaviors and keep both of you stuck in a negative cycle.

4. **Maintains Clarity on Support**
Boundaries define what kind of help you are willing to offer (e.g., emotional support, helping find treatment) versus what you're not (e.g., giving money, covering for their behavior). This clarity prevents confusion and emotional manipulation.

5. **Facilitates Recovery**
Boundaries can motivate the addicted person to seek help. When they recognize that their actions have limits and consequences, they may be more inclined to pursue treatment. Boundaries are a form of tough love that signals you care but won't enable harmful behavior.

6. **Prevents Financial and Legal Strain**
Addiction can sometimes lead to financial or legal issues. Boundaries help protect you from being dragged into these problems, preserving your own stability and protecting against becoming entangled in their consequences.

7. **Fosters Respect and Dignity**
Boundaries can also reinforce the idea that everyone deserves respect, both the addicted person and yourself. Setting clear expectations of behavior fosters healthier interactions and mutual respect.

Boundaries are essential to protect both yourself and your loved one from the toxic effects of addiction, enabling you to support them in a healthier, more constructive way.

by Noelle Rousseau

I wish someone would have told me that sacrificing my boundaries in the name of empathy wasn't noble .
I wish they would've warned me that all it would do is make me a safe house for other people's demons .
I think empathy has to be taught in two parts.
How to put yourself in someone else's shoes and see the hurt they were given that made them hurt you & how to understand that you still don't deserve what they're doing .
Their scars are no excuse for the wound they give to you .
Their inability to heal is not something you can fix .
If you give them excuses and safe places for their darkness instead of demanding they do better,
the only thing you are teaching them is that you will put up with it .
We want to live in a world where hurt people don't hurt people .
But the reality is, that starts with standing up for yourself and not accepting disrespect .
You choose to heal.
You choose to take the darkness the world gave you and still be the light.
You choose kindness despite the pain you received .

They can too.

What boundaries have I set for my loved one and how to I feel about them?

_____
_____
_____
_____
_____
_____
_____
_____
_____

How do I respond when those boundaries are challenged?

_____
_____
_____
_____
_____
_____
_____
_____
_____
_____

Reflection:

Tips on maintaining boundaries

1. Clearly Define Your Boundaries

Take time to reflect on what behaviors you will and will not accept. Be specific and realistic about your limits. For example, you might set a boundary like, "I won't give you money, but I will help you find treatment options."

2. Communicate Boundaries Clearly

Once you've established your boundaries, communicate them to your loved one in a calm, direct, and compassionate manner. Make sure they understand what your limits are and what the consequences will be if those limits are crossed. You may have to write them down on paper to refer to if your loved one needs to be reminded. Texting those boundaries is also a good idea. These boundaries are not open for emotional negotiation.

3. Stay Consistent

This is a biggie, the linch pin on whether your boundary setting works or doesn't work. Consistency is key. If you waver on your boundaries, it sends mixed signals and may encourage manipulative behavior. Stick to your boundaries even if it's uncomfortable or your loved one pushes back.

4. Follow Through with Consequences

If your boundary is crossed, enforce the consequence you've communicated. For example, if you've said you won't lend money and they ask for it, remind them of your boundary and don't give in. DO NOT GIVE IN. Without consequences, boundaries lose their effectiveness.

5. Practice Self-Care

Maintaining boundaries with a loved one struggling with addiction is emotionally draining. Make sure you're taking care of yourself—whether it's through therapy, support groups, hobbies, or simply taking time for yourself to decompress. Healthy boundaries start with self-care. Repeat that. Healthy boundaries begin with self-care. Give yourself that much needed break from the chaos.

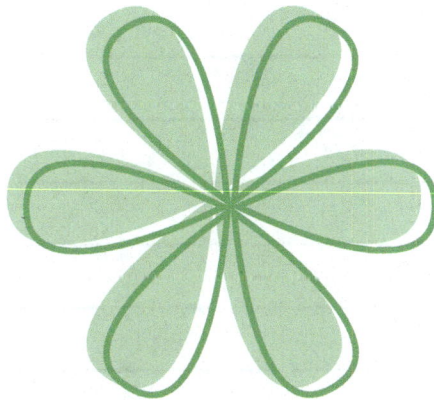

Notes

_____Date

_____

_____

_____

_____

_____

_____

_____

_____

_____

_____

_____

_____

_____

_____

_____

_____

_____

_____

_____

_____

Write 3 things you are grateful for:

1 _____

2 _____

3 _____

What lessons has this experience taught me about myself:

_____

_____

_____

_____

_____

_____

_____

_____

_____

Who or what has been a source of support:

_____

_____

_____

Notes

Date _____

What am I struggling to accept?

How would letting go of certain expectations change my emotional experience?

Write a letter of acceptance to accept.

Write a letter of acceptance to yourself, acknowledging that the situation is beyond your control.

_____

_____

_____

_____

_____

_____

_____

_____

_____

_____

_____

_____

_____

_____

_____

_____

_____

_____

So far, how have I been resilient?

What small steps can I take to foster hope in the future?

Notes

Date _____

Who can I turn to when things feel overwhelming?

_____
_____
_____
_____
_____
_____
_____
_____

How can I ask for help when I need it?

_____
_____
_____
_____
_____
_____
_____
_____

List of supportive people and resources

_____ _____
_____ _____
_____ _____
_____ _____
_____ _____
_____ _____
_____ _____

Notes

Quotes & Affirmations

Here are some powerful quotes and affirmations related to healing, strength, and perseverance. Use whichever ones feel real to you and write them down. Then, repeat them out loud daily. If you find other quotes and affirmations online, add them to your notes. It will help to retrain you brain to think positively. And when you think positively, you will feel positive! It takes approximately 21 days to form a new habit. So, start today! Why wait?

Healing

"Healing takes time, and asking for help is a courageous step."
– Mariska Hargitay

"Healing doesn't mean the damage never existed. It means the damage no longer controls our lives."
– Akshay Dubey

"You have the power to heal your life, and you need to know that."
– Louise Hay

"Healing is not linear, and it's okay to not be okay all the time."
-Anonymous

Affirmation: "I give myself permission to heal and move forward, one step at a time."

Strength

"You never know how strong you are until being strong is your only choice." – Bob Marley

"Strength grows in the moments when you think you can't go on but keep going anyway."
-Ed Mylett

"Out of suffering have emerged the strongest souls; the most massive characters are seared with scars." – Kahlil Gibran

"Do not pray for an easy life; pray for the strength to endure a difficult one."
– Bruce Lee

Affirmation: "I am stronger than I think, and I have the power to overcome any challenge."

Perseverance

"It always seems impossible until it's done."
– Nelson Mandela

"Perseverance is not a long race; it is many short races one after another."
– Walter Elliot

"Success is not final, failure is not fatal: It is the courage to continue that counts."
– Winston Churchill

"Fall seven times, stand up eight."
– Japanese Proverb

Affirmation: "I have the resilience and determination to keep moving forward, no matter how tough the journey gets."

Combination of Healing, Strength, & Perseverance

"The human capacity for burden is like bamboo— far more flexible than you'd ever believe at first glance." – Jodi Picoult

"The wound is the place where the Light enters you." – Rumi

"Scars are not signs of weakness, they are signs of survival and endurance."
– Rodney A. Winters

Affirmation: "I embrace my healing, trust my strength, and honor my perseverance through all of life's challenges."

Minfulness Practices

Here are some simple and effective mindfulness practices to help you stay grounded, reduce stress, and cultivate a sense of presence in your daily life. These exercises may be uncomfortable at first, especially when they are attempted in the midst of the latest drama your addicted loved one has created. But persevere. It will pay off. Promise.

1. Mindful Breathing

Focus on your breath to anchor yourself in the present moment. This practice can help calm your mind and reduce stress.

How to Practice: Sit or lie down in a comfortable position. Close your eyes and take a deep breath in through your nose for a count of four, hold for four, and exhale for four. Pay attention to the sensation of the breath entering and leaving your body. When your mind wanders, gently guide it back to your breathing.
Duration: 5–10 minutes.

2. Body Scan Meditation

A body scan is a way to bring awareness to different parts of your body and release physical tension.
How to Practice: Lie down in a quiet place. Close your eyes and focus on your breath for a minute. Then, slowly bring attention to different parts of your body, starting from your toes and working your way up to your head. Notice any sensations, tension, or discomfort, and consciously release tension as you move from one body part to the next.
Duration: 10–20 minutes.

3. Mindful Eating

This practice encourages you to slow down and fully experience your food, bringing awareness to the act of eating. It can open a whole new world for you. And it's fun.

How to Practice: Choose a meal or snack. Before you eat, take a moment to observe the food—its colors, textures, and smells. Eat slowly, paying attention to the taste, texture, and sensations of each bite. Chew thoroughly and notice the feeling of fullness. Avoid distractions like TV or phones while eating.
Duration: During a meal or snack.

4. Gratitude Practice

Practicing gratitude helps shift your focus from what's missing to what you already have. When in doubt, be grateful for something.

How to Practice: Each day, write down three things you're grateful for. They can be simple, like a warm bed, a conversation with a friend, or even the ability to breathe. Reflect on why you are thankful for each thing and how it positively affects your life.
Duration: 5 minutes daily.

5. Five Senses Exercise

This exercise is great for grounding yourself in the present moment, especially when you're feeling overwhelmed. And it can be fun.

How to Practice: Pause for a moment and focus on each of your five senses. Name:
5 things you can see,
4 things you can feel,
3 things you can hear,
2 things you can smell,
1 thing you can taste.
This brings your awareness back to the present and helps quiet your mind.
Duration: 5–10 minutes.

6. Walking Meditation

Walking meditation is a way to combine movement with mindfulness, which can be especially helpful for those who find it hard to sit still.

How to Practice: Find a quiet place to walk slowly. Focus on the sensation of your feet touching the ground, the movement of your legs, and the rhythm of your steps. Pay attention to your surroundings, including sounds, smells, and sights, but return your focus to your steps when your mind starts to wander.
Duration: 10–20 minutes.

7. Mindful Observation

This practice helps you reconnect with the beauty of your environment by focusing fully on a single object.

How to Practice: Choose an object in your environment, like a flower, tree, or even a cup of tea. Observe it closely for a few minutes. Notice its colors, shapes, textures, and how it interacts with light. The goal is to focus completely on the object, bringing your awareness to its details.
Duration: 3–5 minutes.

8. Loving-Kindness Meditation (Metta Meditation)

This practice involves cultivating compassion and love for yourself and others.

How to Practice: Sit quietly, close your eyes, and take a few deep breaths. Begin by silently repeating the following phrases: "May I be happy. May I be healthy. May I be safe. May I live with ease." After a few minutes, extend these wishes to others, such as loved ones, friends, or even difficult people in your life. You can say, "May you be happy. May you be healthy. May you be safe. May you live with ease."
Duration: 10–15 minutes.

9. Mindful Stretching or Yoga

Incorporating gentle stretching or yoga helps you connect with your body and breath while relieving tension.

How to Practice: Choose a few simple stretches or yoga poses. As you stretch, focus on your breath and the sensation in each muscle group. Move slowly and mindfully, paying attention to how your body feels during each movement.
Duration: 10–20 minutes.

10. Mindful Listening

This practice helps you develop a deeper sense of presence in your interactions with others.

How to Practice: The next time you are in conversation, focus entirely on what the other person is saying without planning your response or allowing your mind to wander. Notice their tone, body language, and words. By being fully present, you can engage more deeply and compassionately.
Duration: During conversations.

If none of these mindfulness practices appeal to you, the Internet is loaded with exercises that should. You have a whole world of information at your fingertips. Make it work for you!

Notes

Reflections on Growth

Looking back, in what ways have I grown?

_____

_____

_____

_____

_____

_____

_____

_____

_____

What plositive changes have come from this experience?

_____

_____

_____

_____

_____

_____

_____

_____

_____

_____

Notes

What do I hope to gain from journaling through this experience?

_____

_____

_____

_____

_____

_____

_____

_____

_____

_____

_____

_____

_____

_____

_____

_____

Set some self-care goals for yourself:

_____

_____

_____

_____

_____

_____

_____

_____

_____

_____

_____

_____

_____

_____

_____

_____

_____

Date:

How am I feeling today: Happy   Resentful   Peaceful   Sad   Numb
Furious   Defeated   Guilty   Angry   Depressed   Empty   Anxious
Inspired   Helpless   Confused   Held hostage   Isolated

(Circle as many as are accurate)

Who or what triggered these emotions?

How did I react?

What emotions am I strugling with most now?

How has my child's addiction impacted me emotionally?

_____
_____
_____
_____
_____
_____
_____
_____
_____
_____
_____
_____
_____
_____
_____
_____
_____

How can I handle it differently next time?

_____
_____
_____
_____
_____
_____
_____
_____
_____
_____
_____
_____
_____

Notes

In what ways do I feel responsible for my loved one's addiction?

_____
_____
_____
_____
_____
_____
_____
_____

How can I startt to let go of feelings of guilt or blame?

_____
_____
_____
_____
_____
_____
_____
_____

I am full of compassion towards myself.
I release the stories that make me feel small.
I hold space for myself in this healing process.
I deserve happiness

Notes

What uncertainties am I coping with today?

_____

_____

_____

_____

_____

_____

**What are the things within my control and what can
I do about them?**

_____

_____

_____

_____

_____

_____

_____

Refection Exercise

Write down both your fears and your hopes, then identify actionable steps to reduce the anxiety of uncertainties. i.e. yoga, exercise, refuse to answer the phone, etc.

What have I done for myself today?

It what ways can I promote more self-compassion?

Self –Care Check List

Circle as many as needed

Relaxing bath   Hobby   Write an email

Exercise   Relaxation techniques

Support group   Counseling   Movie

Journal writing   Walk   Day trip

Talk with a friend   Out to eat

Yoga   Read   Watch TV

Add more:

_____

_____

_____

by Noelle Rousseau

I wish someone would have told me that sacrificing my boundaries in the name of empathy wasn't noble .
I wish they would've warned me that all it would do is make me a safe house for other people's demons .
I think empathy has to be taught in two parts.
How to put yourself in someone else's shoes and see the hurt they were given that made them hurt you & how to understand that you still don't deserve what they're doing .
Their scars are no excuse for the wound they give to you .
Their inability to heal is not something you can fix .
If you give them excuses and safe places for their darkness instead of demanding they do better,
the only thing you are teaching them is that you will put up with it .
We want to live in a world where hurt people don't hurt people .
But the reality is, that starts with standing up for yourself and not accepting disrespect .
You choose to heal.
You choose to take the darkness the world gave you and still be the light.
You choose kindness despite the pain you received .

They can too.

What boundaries have I set for my loved one and how to I feel about them?

_____
_____
_____
_____
_____
_____
_____
_____
_____

How do I respond when those boundaries are challenged?

_____
_____
_____
_____
_____
_____
_____
_____
_____

Reflection:

Tips on maintaining boundaries

1. Clearly Define Your Boundaries
Take time to reflect on what behaviors you will and will not accept. Be specific and realistic about your limits. For example, you might set a boundary like, "I won't give you money, but I will help you find treatment options."

2. Communicate Boundaries Clearly
Once you've established your boundaries, communicate them to your loved one in a calm, direct, and compassionate manner. Make sure they understand what your limits are and what the consequences will be if those limits are crossed. You may have to write them down on paper to refer to if your loved one needs to be reminded. Texting those boundaries is also a good idea. These boundaries are not open for emotional negotiation.

3. Stay Consistent
This is a biggie, the linch pin on whether your boundary setting works or doesn't work. Consistency is key. If you waver on your boundaries, it sends mixed signals and may encourage manipulative behavior. Stick to your boundaries even if it's uncomfortable or your loved one pushes back.

4. Follow Through with Consequences
If your boundary is crossed, enforce the consequence you've communicated. For example, if you've said you won't lend money and they ask for it, remind them of your boundary and don't give in. DO NOT GIVE IN. Without consequences, boundaries lose their effectiveness.

5. Practice Self-Care
Maintaining boundaries with a loved one struggling with addiction is emotionally draining. Make sure you're taking care of yourself—whether it's through therapy, support groups, hobbies, or simply taking time for yourself to decompress. Healthy boundaries start with self-care. Repeat that. Healthy boundaries begin with self-care. Give yourself that much needed break from the chaos.

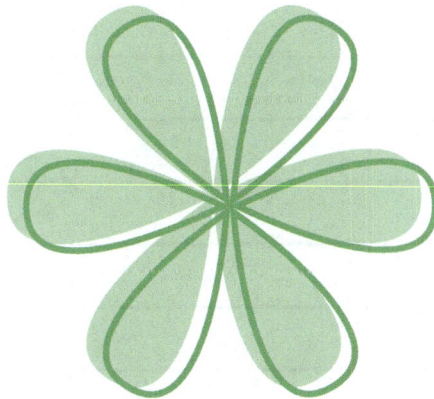

Notes

_____Date
_____
_____
_____
_____
_____
_____
_____
_____
_____
_____
_____
_____
_____
_____
_____
_____
_____
_____
_____
_____

Write 3 things you are grateful for:

1 _____

2 _____

3 _____

What lessons has this experience taught me about myself:

_____

_____

_____

_____

_____

_____

_____

_____

Who or what has been a source of support:

_____

_____

_____

Notes

_____ Date

What am I struggling to accept?

_____

_____

_____

_____

_____

_____

_____

How would letting go of certain expectations change my emotional experience?

_____

_____

_____

_____

_____

_____

Write a letter of acceptance to yourself, acknowledging that the situation is beyond your control.

_____

_____

_____

_____

_____

_____

_____

_____

_____

_____

_____

_____

_____

_____

_____

_____

_____

So far, how have I been resilient?

What small steps can I take to foster hope in the future?

Notes

Date

Who can I turn to when things feel overwhelming?

_____

_____

_____

_____

_____

_____

_____

How can I ask for help when I need it?

_____

_____

_____

_____

_____

_____

_____

List of supportive people and resources

_____ _____

_____ _____

_____ _____

_____ _____

_____ _____

_____ _____

_____ _____

Notes

Quotes & Affirmations

Here are some powerful quotes and affirmations related to healing, strength, and perseverance. Use whichever ones feel real to you and write them down. Then, repeat them out loud daily. If you find other quotes and affirmations online, add them to your notes. It will help to retrain you brain to think positively. And when you think positively, you will feel positive! It takes approximately 21 days to form a new habit. So, start today! Why wait?

Healing

"Healing takes time, and asking for help is a courageous step."
– Mariska Hargitay

"Healing doesn't mean the damage never existed. It means the damage no longer controls our lives."
– Akshay Dubey

"You have the power to heal your life, and you need to know that."
– Louise Hay

"Healing is not linear, and it's okay to not be okay all the time."
-Anonymous

Affirmation: "I give myself permission to heal and move forward, one step at a time."

Strength

"You never know how strong you are until being strong is your only choice." – Bob Marley

"Strength grows in the moments when you think you can't go on but keep going anyway."
-Ed Mylett

"Out of suffering have emerged the strongest souls; the most massive characters are seared with scars." – Kahlil Gibran

"Do not pray for an easy life; pray for the strength to endure a difficult one."
– Bruce Lee

Affirmation: "I am stronger than I think, and I have the power to overcome any challenge."

Perseverance

"It always seems impossible until it's done."
– Nelson Mandela

"Perseverance is not a long race; it is many short races one after another."
– Walter Elliot

"Success is not final, failure is not fatal: It is the courage to continue that counts."
– Winston Churchill

"Fall seven times, stand up eight."
– Japanese Proverb

Affirmation: "I have the resilience and determination to keep moving forward, no matter how tough the journey gets."

Combination of Healing, Strength, & Perseverance

"The human capacity for burden is like bamboo—far more flexible than you'd ever believe at first glance." – Jodi Picoult

"The wound is the place where the Light enters you." – Rumi

"Scars are not signs of weakness, they are signs of survival and endurance."
– Rodney A. Winters

Affirmation: "I embrace my healing, trust my strength, and honor my perseverance through all of life's challenges."

Minfulness Practices

Here are some simple and effective mindfulness practices to help you stay grounded, reduce stress, and cultivate a sense of presence in your daily life. These exercises may be uncomfortable at first, especially when they are attempted in the midst of the latest drama your addicted loved one has created. But persevere. It will pay off. Promise.

1. Mindful Breathing

Focus on your breath to anchor yourself in the present moment. This practice can help calm your mind and reduce stress.

How to Practice: Sit or lie down in a comfortable position. Close your eyes and take a deep breath in through your nose for a count of four, hold for four, and exhale for four. Pay attention to the sensation of the breath entering and leaving your body. When your mind wanders, gently guide it back to your breathing.
Duration: 5–10 minutes.

2. Body Scan Meditation

A body scan is a way to bring awareness to different parts of your body and release physical tension.
How to Practice: Lie down in a quiet place. Close your eyes and focus on your breath for a minute. Then, slowly bring attention to different parts of your body, starting from your toes and working your way up to your head. Notice any sensations, tension, or discomfort, and consciously release tension as you move from one body part to the next.
Duration: 10–20 minutes.

3. Mindful Eating

This practice encourages you to slow down and fully experience your food, bringing awareness to the act of eating. It can open a whole new world for you. And it's fun.

How to Practice: Choose a meal or snack. Before you eat, take a moment to observe the food—its colors, textures, and smells. Eat slowly, paying attention to the taste, texture, and sensations of each bite. Chew thoroughly and notice the feeling of fullness. Avoid distractions like TV or phones while eating.
Duration: During a meal or snack.

4. Gratitude Practice

Practicing gratitude helps shift your focus from what's missing to what you already have. When in doubt, be grateful for something.

How to Practice: Each day, write down three things you're grateful for. They can be simple, like a warm bed, a conversation with a friend, or even the ability to breathe. Reflect on why you are thankful for each thing and how it positively affects your life.
Duration: 5 minutes daily.

5. Five Senses Exercise

This exercise is great for grounding yourself in the present moment, especially when you're feeling overwhelmed. And it can be fun.

How to Practice: Pause for a moment and focus on each of your five senses. Name:
5 things you can see,
4 things you can feel,
3 things you can hear,
2 things you can smell,
1 thing you can taste.
This brings your awareness back to the present and helps quiet your mind.
Duration: 5–10 minutes.

6. Walking Meditation

Walking meditation is a way to combine movement with mindfulness, which can be especially helpful for those who find it hard to sit still.

How to Practice: Find a quiet place to walk slowly. Focus on the sensation of your feet touching the ground, the movement of your legs, and the rhythm of your steps. Pay attention to your surroundings, including sounds, smells, and sights, but return your focus to your steps when your mind starts to wander.
Duration: 10–20 minutes.

7. Mindful Observation

This practice helps you reconnect with the beauty of your environment by focusing fully on a single object.

How to Practice: Choose an object in your environment, like a flower, tree, or even a cup of tea. Observe it closely for a few minutes. Notice its colors, shapes, textures, and how it interacts with light. The goal is to focus completely on the object, bringing your awareness to its details.
Duration: 3–5 minutes.

8. Loving-Kindness Meditation (Metta Meditation)

This practice involves cultivating compassion and love for yourself and others.

How to Practice: Sit quietly, close your eyes, and take a few deep breaths. Begin by silently repeating the following phrases: "May I be happy. May I be healthy. May I be safe. May I live with ease." After a few minutes, extend these wishes to others, such as loved ones, friends, or even difficult people in your life. You can say, "May you be happy. May you be healthy. May you be safe. May you live with ease."
Duration: 10–15 minutes.

9. Mindful Stretching or Yoga

Incorporating gentle stretching or yoga helps you connect with your body and breath while relieving tension.

How to Practice: Choose a few simple stretches or yoga poses. As you stretch, focus on your breath and the sensation in each muscle group. Move slowly and mindfully, paying attention to how your body feels during each movement.
Duration: 10–20 minutes.

10. Mindful Listening

This practice helps you develop a deeper sense of presence in your interactions with others.

How to Practice: The next time you are in conversation, focus entirely on what the other person is saying without planning your response or allowing your mind to wander. Notice their tone, body language, and words. By being fully present, you can engage more deeply and compassionately.
Duration: During conversations.

If none of these mindfulness practices appeal to you, the Internet is loaded with exercises that should. You have a whole world of information at your fingertips. Make it work for you!

Notes

Reflections on Growth

Looking back, in what ways have I grown?

_____

_____

_____

_____

_____

_____

_____

_____

What plositive changes have come from this experience?

_____

_____

_____

_____

_____

_____

_____

_____

_____

Notes

Day 7

What do I hope to gain from journaling through this experience?

Set some self-care goals for yourself:

Date:

How am I feeling today: Happy   Resentful   Peaceful   Sad   Numb
Furious   Defeated   Guilty   Angry   Depressed   Empty   Anxious
Inspired   Helpless   Confused   Held hostage   Isolated

(Circle as many as are accurate)

Who or what triggered these emotions?

How did I react?

What emotions am I strugling with most now?

How has my child's addiction impacted me emotionally?

_____
_____
_____
_____
_____
_____
_____
_____
_____
_____
_____
_____
_____
_____
_____

How can I handle it differently next time?

_____
_____
_____
_____
_____
_____
_____
_____
_____
_____
_____
_____
_____

Notes

In what ways do I feel responsible for my loved one's addiction?

_____

_____

_____

_____

_____

_____

_____

_____

How can I startt to let go of feelings of guilt or blame?

_____

_____

_____

_____

_____

_____

_____

_____

I am full of compassion towards myself.
I release the stories that make me feel small.
I hold space for myself in this healing process.
I deserve happiness

Notes

What uncertainties am I coping with today?

_____

_____

_____

_____

_____

_____

What are the things within my control and what can I do about them?

_____

_____

_____

_____

_____

_____

Refection Exercise

Write down both your fears and your hopes, then identify actionable steps to reduce the anxiety of uncertainties. i.e. yoga, exercise, refuse to answer the phone, etc.

_____

_____

_____

_____

_____

_____

_____

_____

_____

_____

_____

_____

What have I done for myself today?

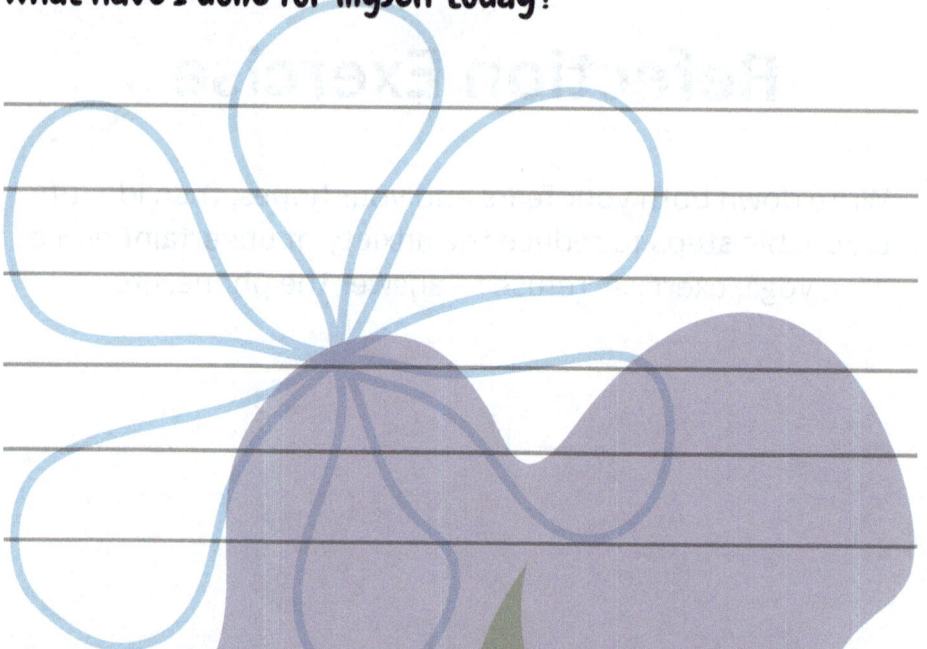

_____

_____

_____

_____

_____

_____

It what ways can I promote more self-compassion?

_____

_____

_____

_____

_____

_____

_____

Self -Care Check List

Circle as many as needed

Relaxing bath   Hobby   Write an email

Exercise   Relaxation techniques

Support group   Counseling   Movie

Journal writing   Walk   Day trip

Talk with a friend   Out to eat

Yoga   Read   Watch TV

Add more:

_____

_____

_____

by Noelle Rousseau

I wish someone would have told me that sacrificing my
boundaries in the name of empathy wasn't noble .
I wish they would've warned me that all it would do is
make me a safe house for other people's demons .
I think empathy has to be taught in two parts.
How to put yourself in someone else's shoes and see the
hurt they were given that made them hurt you & how to
understand that you still don't deserve what they're
doing .
Their scars are no excuse for the wound they give to you .
Their inability to heal is not something you can fix .
If you give them excuses and safe places for their
darkness instead of demanding they do better,
the only thing you are teaching them is that you will put
up with it .
We want to live in a world where hurt people don't hurt
people .
But the reality is, that starts with standing up for yourself
and not accepting disrespect .
You choose to heal.
You choose to take the darkness the world gave you and
still be the light.
You choose kindness despite the pain you received .

They can too.

What boundaries have I set for my loved one and how to I feel about them?

_____
_____
_____
_____
_____
_____
_____
_____
_____

How do I respond when those boundaries are challenged?

_____
_____
_____
_____
_____
_____
_____
_____
_____
_____

Reflection:

Tips on maintaining boundaries

1. Clearly Define Your Boundaries

Take time to reflect on what behaviors you will and will not accept. Be specific and realistic about your limits. For example, you might set a boundary like, "I won't give you money, but I will help you find treatment options."

2. Communicate Boundaries Clearly

Once you've established your boundaries, communicate them to your loved one in a calm, direct, and compassionate manner. Make sure they understand what your limits are and what the consequences will be if those limits are crossed. You may have to write them down on paper to refer to if your loved one needs to be reminded. Texting those boundaries is also a good idea. These boundaries are not open for emotional negotiation.

3. Stay Consistent

This is a biggie, the linch pin on whether your boundary setting works or doesn't work. Consistency is key. If you waver on your boundaries, it sends mixed signals and may encourage manipulative behavior. Stick to your boundaries even if it's uncomfortable or your loved one pushes back.

4. Follow Through with Consequences

If your boundary is crossed, enforce the consequence you've communicated. For example, if you've said you won't lend money and they ask for it, remind them of your boundary and don't give in. DO NOT GIVE IN. Without consequences, boundaries lose their effectiveness.

5. Practice Self-Care

Maintaining boundaries with a loved one struggling with addiction is emotionally draining. Make sure you're taking care of yourself—whether it's through therapy, support groups, hobbies, or simply taking time for yourself to decompress. Healthy boundaries start with self-care. Repeat that. Healthy boundaries begin with self-care. Give yourself that much needed break from the chaos.

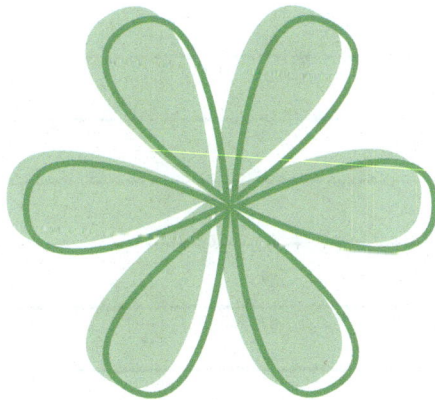

Notes

_____Date
_____
_____
_____
_____
_____
_____
_____
_____
_____
_____
_____
_____
_____
_____
_____
_____
_____
_____
_____
_____

Write 3 things you are grateful for:

1

2

3

What lessons has this experience taught me about myself:

Who or what has been a source of support:

Notes

Date _____

What am I struggling to accept?

How would letting go of certain expectations change my emotional experience?

Write a letter of acceptance to yourself, acknowledging that the situation is beyond your control.

_____

_____

_____

_____

_____

_____

_____

_____

_____

_____

_____

_____

_____

_____

_____

_____

So far, how have I been resilient?

What small steps can I take to foster hope in the future?

Notes

Date _____

_____
_____
_____
_____
_____
_____
_____
_____
_____
_____
_____
_____
_____
_____
_____
_____
_____
_____
_____
_____

Who can I turn to when things feel overwhelming?

_____

_____

_____

_____

_____

_____

_____

_____

How can I ask for help when I need it?

_____

_____

_____

_____

_____

_____

_____

List of supportive people and resources

_____   _____

_____   _____

_____   _____

_____   _____

_____   _____

_____   _____

_____   _____

Notes

_____

_____

_____

_____

_____

_____

_____

_____

_____

_____

_____

_____

_____

_____

_____

_____

Quotes & Affirmations

Here are some powerful quotes and affirmations related to healing, strength, and perseverance. Use whichever ones feel real to you and write them down. Then, repeat them out loud daily. If you find other quotes and affirmations online, add them to your notes. It will help to retrain you brain to think positively. And when you think positively, you will feel positive! It takes approximately 21 days to form a new habit. So, start today! Why wait?

Healing

"Healing takes time, and asking for help is a courageous step."
– Mariska Hargitay

"Healing doesn't mean the damage never existed. It means the damage no longer controls our lives."
– Akshay Dubey

"You have the power to heal your life, and you need to know that."
– Louise Hay

"Healing is not linear, and it's okay to not be okay all the time."
-Anonymous

Affirmation: "I give myself permission to heal and move forward, one step at a time."

Strength

"You never know how strong you are until being strong is your only choice." – Bob Marley

"Strength grows in the moments when you think you can't go on but keep going anyway."
-Ed Mylett

"Out of suffering have emerged the strongest souls; the most massive characters are seared with scars." – Kahlil Gibran

"Do not pray for an easy life; pray for the strength to endure a difficult one."
– Bruce Lee

Affirmation: "I am stronger than I think, and I have the power to overcome any challenge."

Perseverance

"It always seems impossible until it's done."
– Nelson Mandela

"Perseverance is not a long race; it is many short races one after another."
– Walter Elliot

"Success is not final, failure is not fatal: It is the courage to continue that counts."
– Winston Churchill

"Fall seven times, stand up eight."
– Japanese Proverb

Affirmation: "I have the resilience and determination to keep moving forward, no matter how tough the journey gets."

Combination of Healing, Strength, & Perseverance

"The human capacity for burden is like bamboo—far more flexible than you'd ever believe at first glance." – Jodi Picoult

"The wound is the place where the Light enters you." – Rumi

"Scars are not signs of weakness, they are signs of survival and endurance."
– Rodney A. Winters

Affirmation: "I embrace my healing, trust my strength, and honor my perseverance through all of life's challenges."

Minfulness Practices

Here are some simple and effective mindfulness practices to help you stay grounded, reduce stress, and cultivate a sense of presence in your daily life. These exercises may be uncomfortable at first, especially when they are attempted in the midst of the latest drama your addicted loved one has created. But persevere. It will pay off. Promise.

1. Mindful Breathing
Focus on your breath to anchor yourself in the present moment. This practice can help calm your mind and reduce stress.

How to Practice: Sit or lie down in a comfortable position. Close your eyes and take a deep breath in through your nose for a count of four, hold for four, and exhale for four. Pay attention to the sensation of the breath entering and leaving your body. When your mind wanders, gently guide it back to your breathing.
Duration: 5–10 minutes.

2. Body Scan Meditation
A body scan is a way to bring awareness to different parts of your body and release physical tension.
How to Practice: Lie down in a quiet place. Close your eyes and focus on your breath for a minute. Then, slowly bring attention to different parts of your body, starting from your toes and working your way up to your head. Notice any sensations, tension, or discomfort, and consciously release tension as you move from one body part to the next.
Duration: 10–20 minutes.

3. Mindful Eating

This practice encourages you to slow down and fully experience your food, bringing awareness to the act of eating. It can open a whole new world for you. And it's fun.

How to Practice: Choose a meal or snack. Before you eat, take a moment to observe the food—its colors, textures, and smells. Eat slowly, paying attention to the taste, texture, and sensations of each bite. Chew thoroughly and notice the feeling of fullness. Avoid distractions like TV or phones while eating.
Duration: During a meal or snack.

4. Gratitude Practice

Practicing gratitude helps shift your focus from what's missing to what you already have. When in doubt, be grateful for something.

How to Practice: Each day, write down three things you're grateful for. They can be simple, like a warm bed, a conversation with a friend, or even the ability to breathe. Reflect on why you are thankful for each thing and how it positively affects your life.
Duration: 5 minutes daily.

5. Five Senses Exercise

This exercise is great for grounding yourself in the present moment, especially when you're feeling overwhelmed. And it can be fun.

How to Practice: Pause for a moment and focus on each of your five senses. Name:
5 things you can see,
4 things you can feel,
3 things you can hear,
2 things you can smell,
1 thing you can taste.
This brings your awareness back to the present and helps quiet your mind.
Duration: 5–10 minutes.

6. Walking Meditation

Walking meditation is a way to combine movement with mindfulness, which can be especially helpful for those who find it hard to sit still.

How to Practice: Find a quiet place to walk slowly. Focus on the sensation of your feet touching the ground, the movement of your legs, and the rhythm of your steps. Pay attention to your surroundings, including sounds, smells, and sights, but return your focus to your steps when your mind starts to wander.
Duration: 10–20 minutes.

7. Mindful Observation

This practice helps you reconnect with the beauty of your environment by focusing fully on a single object.

How to Practice: Choose an object in your environment, like a flower, tree, or even a cup of tea. Observe it closely for a few minutes. Notice its colors, shapes, textures, and how it interacts with light. The goal is to focus completely on the object, bringing your awareness to its details.
Duration: 3–5 minutes.

8. Loving-Kindness Meditation (Metta Meditation)

This practice involves cultivating compassion and love for yourself and others.

How to Practice: Sit quietly, close your eyes, and take a few deep breaths. Begin by silently repeating the following phrases: "May I be happy. May I be healthy. May I be safe. May I live with ease." After a few minutes, extend these wishes to others, such as loved ones, friends, or even difficult people in your life. You can say, "May you be happy. May you be healthy. May you be safe. May you live with ease."
Duration: 10–15 minutes.

9. Mindful Stretching or Yoga

Incorporating gentle stretching or yoga helps you connect with your body and breath while relieving tension.

How to Practice: Choose a few simple stretches or yoga poses. As you stretch, focus on your breath and the sensation in each muscle group. Move slowly and mindfully, paying attention to how your body feels during each movement.
Duration: 10–20 minutes.

10. Mindful Listening

This practice helps you develop a deeper sense of presence in your interactions with others.

How to Practice: The next time you are in conversation, focus entirely on what the other person is saying without planning your response or allowing your mind to wander. Notice their tone, body language, and words. By being fully present, you can engage more deeply and compassionately.
Duration: During conversations.

If none of these mindfulness practices appeal to you, the Internet is loaded with exercises that should. You have a whole world of information at your fingertips. Make it work for you!

Notes

Reflections on Growth

Looking back, in what ways have I grown?

_____
_____
_____
_____
_____
_____
_____
_____
_____

What plositive changes have come from this experience?

_____
_____
_____
_____
_____
_____
_____
_____
_____
_____
_____

Notes

Notes

Congratulations!

Now, repeat as needed!

Made in the USA
Las Vegas, NV
29 January 2025